RICK BOYCHUK

RIVER OF GRIT

D1604027

Six Months On The Line At Suncor

FT. McMURRAY, ALBERTA, 1986

© 1996 Duval House Publishing

Canadian Cataloguing in Publication Data
Boychuk, Rick, 1953-
  River of grit

  (Rank 'n file)
    ISBN: 1-895850-48-7

  1. Great Canadian Oil Sands Ltd. Strike, 1986. 2. Strikes and lockouts – Oils sands industry – Alberta. 3. Energy and Chemical Workers Union. 4. Oil sands industry – Alberta. I. Title. II. Series
HD5329.P42 1986 A42 1995   331.89'04655'097123   C95-911109-3

Duval House Publishing gratefully acknowledges the support of the Alberta Foundation for the Arts, the Canada Council, and the Cultural Industries Agreement of Alberta.

Executive Editor: Neil C. Reimer
Cover Design: Kim Johansen, Black Dog Design
Production: Pièce de Résistance Ltée.
Printing: ABC Press Ltd.
PHOTO CREDITS: Pages 4-7, 14-15, 30-31, 48-49, 66-67, 70-71, 78-79, 112-113, 132-133, 140-141 are courtesy of the Fort McMurray Today. All other photographs are courtesy of members of CEPU Local 707.

Duval House Publishing
18228 - 102 Ave
Edmonton, Alberta
T5S 1S7

CONTENTS

Experience is the name everyone gives to their mistakes.

OSCAR WILDE

A desperate disease requires a dangerous remedy.

GUY FAWKES

Many MIOW workers were unprepared for a lengthy labour dispute. Management, however, had organized for at least a six-month siege.

OVERLEAF PAGES 4 & 5: Suncor's front gates are taken over by a large RCMP contingent that some people believe was a riot squad preparing for security duties at Expo '86 in Vancouver.

OVERLEAF PAGES 6 & 7: Picketing at the front gate, from l to r, Kirk McRae, Brent Craig, Keith Barrington, Matt Rogers, Rod Serediak, Ken Snook, Winston Piercy, Keith Leamon, Bill Roberts, Todd Jackson.

CHAPTER ONE

THE SETUP

BY THE TIME the first picket lines were thrown up at the gates of Suncor's oil sands plant north of Fort McMurray at midnight April 30, 1986, company management had laid in everything needed for a long seige. They'd consulted lawyers, fortified the gates, beefed-up the security force, briefed their bus transportation contractor, hired a professional photographer and had flown in staff from across the continent to run the plant. At the camp inside the plant perimeter, the video library had been stocked with films ranging from science fiction to comedy. Aerobics classes had been organized, floor hockey teams were being formed and the Canadians/Rangers NHL playoffs were on the big screen in the recreation centre at night. There was both precision and purpose within the plant and among management personnel, two qualities that had never before seemed to be much in focus. A great deal was at stake. Ron Wood, then head of the plant's human resources department, said that he and his colleagues had basically "bet our jobs" that they could run the mine and refinery and manage the dispute, however long it was going to take.

Aside from the quotidian job of producing light synthetic crude oil, one of the first tasks management undertook was to gather information necessary for an injunction. Gene Bacon, a former member of the union's executive who had joined Suncor staff and was on the company's negotiating team, said everybody that "had to be at the plant was brought in on April 30 so nothing had to come through the gate for the first couple of days. The camp at the time could hold about 1400." So although for production purposes there was no reason to bring anybody across the picket line, the company did need someone to cross the line in order to obtain an injunction. The editor of the plant's in-house newsletter explained it all to staffers on May 2: "When picketers block access to company property, the company requests a court injunction from a judge to regain access on the grounds that conducting of company business is being interfered with. To get that injunction, the company has to provide the judge with sufficient, concrete evidence that shows its ability to conduct business as usual is being hindered by the picketers. At this point, Suncor is collecting evidence to get the injunction."

That passage was written on May 1, the day the dispute began. Most of the lucky folks who were in the vehicles Suncor attempted to send across the line that first day were secretaries and janitors. It wasn't that the place was such a mess and that letters needed to be written and that an urgent call had gone out for janitors and secretaries at any cost, at any peril. What was needed were pictures and eyewitness accounts of picketers attempting to block employees from coming in, and janitors and secretaries would, apparently, do nicely. Those pictures and eyewitness accounts were duly obtained and subsequently used in court.

Thirteen affidavits were presented to the court by company lawyers to buttress Suncor's demand for an injunction. The affidavit of security guard Randy Rachinsky was typical. Rachinsky said that on May 1 he saw a picketer strike a Proserve Cleaners van that was attempting to enter the plant site. He also said that a picketer told him "I hope you have house insurance," and "I'll take a picture of you with black eyes." There was much more, most of it similar in tone and nature. The court didn't see the humour in any of the remarks attributed to the picketers. The injunction was granted, and the company won the first round in what, even then in those early days, was shaping up to be a lengthy battle.

It was a battle that eventually engulfed the entire community of Fort McMurray, a booming city 431 kilometres north of Edmonton that had blossomed to maturity, in less than two decades, from a small, isolated town tucked into the junction of

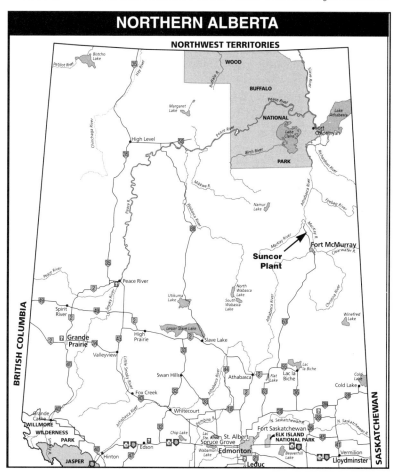

The Suncor plant is located 35 kilometres north of Fort McMurray on the west side of the Athabasca River. Opened in 1967, the plant is designed to produce 26 000 barrels of light synthetic crude a day.

the Athabasca and Clearwater rivers. There'd been other labour disputes at the Suncor oil sands plant north of the city, but this one would shake the city to its foundations. This lockout would last six months and would divide families, skewer neighbourhoods and tear apart friendships. It would drive businesses into bankruptcy, inspire boycotts and provoke mass arrests. It wouldn't attract the media attention that the Gainers' dispute in Edmonton did during what proved to be a long, hot summer of labour unrest across Alberta. But it was easily as costly and, at times, as violent as the lockout at the Peter Pocklington-owned meat packing plant in the provincial capital. Both sides in the Suncor dispute were to say later the fight was inevitable, and that after the tempest was over, the air cleared, and labour relations at the plant became more productive and collaborative than they had ever been. This isn't to suggest that labour/management brawls are vital cleansing processes, but that sometimes a well-fought battle will lead warring factions to reappraise each other. The six-month long dispute at Suncor produced no clear winner; the opponents walloped each other to a standstill. When it was over, both sides had learned a great deal about their own leadership, about their own character flaws, their own mistakes. Management discovered that the union couldn't be broken, and union members realized that the fat and happy days of big raises and the company turning a blind eye to abuses of overtime and high absentee rates were over.

Graham and Colleen Waterman.

This is the story of the labour dispute, a conflict that played itself out in the spring, summer and fall of 1986, a dispute fought by Alberta rules and provoked by international commodity prices. It's the story of a lockout in a one-industry town and the effect that the quarrel had on the community and on the company. Most of all it is the story of the impact that battle had on the men and women and families who spent six months waging a bare-knuckle fight for their jobs.

There are no villains in this story. There are only well-meaning people who sometimes made mistakes; who occasionally lost their temper; who from time to time took actions they were later to regret; who at moments showed inspired leadership or great generosity of spirit; and who, in the end, were acting in what they understood to be the best interests of family, union,

Workers and spouses hold up signs to protest the number of police that were brought against them.

employer or community. Both sides fought in earnest and with whatever was at hand. Fortunately no one was seriously injured. But there were plenty of hurtful accusations flung about and reputations were damaged. And those are lingering wounds. Injuries heal. Insults fester forever. The workers on the line that first day had a taste of what was to come when they saw company security officers recording both their actions and their angry comments. Everything they did and said, the company was telling them, was going to be used against them. Threaten to blacken a company man's eyes and the courts and RCMP were going to hear about it. The battle had been joined.

Opinion is ultimately determined by the feelings, and not the intellect.

HERBERT SPENCER

Jerry Snow talks to a Diversified Transport bus driver. Eventually, bringing scabs across the line becomes impossible until an injunction is heard.

OVERLEAF: Busses carrying replacement workers from the Suncor site turn onto Highway 63, while MIOW workers look on and a professional photographer watches the MIOW workers.

CHAPTER TWO

RAIDERS OF THE
RENEGADE ASSOCIATION

DON MARCHAND stepped back into the union president's office at the Suncor oil sands plant in the fall of 1984. He had withdrawn as president of the McMurray Independent Oil Workers Union in 1983, sat out a term and then was voted back into the office of the president in 1984. A pugnacious former oilrig hand, a former member of the Seafarer's International Union who had worked on BC ferries, Marchand had moved to McMurray in 1971 to work in Suncor's top shop as a lube man. He was married and had three kids.

Marchand quickly made his presence felt in the community and at the plant. At the time, the employees belonged to a company association, and Marchand says, from the outset, he was outspoken in his view that the association was making mistakes in negotiations with the company. A year after his arrival a friend suggested he run for shop steward. Marchand did, won, and by

1976 was confident enough in his skills to take aim at the presidency. Again he was successful. He assumed the post at a time when oil prices were starting an upward spiral that, by 1981, would reach almost $40 a barrel. It was a time when overexcited oil company officials were confidently predicting prices would top $100 a barrel by the mid-1990s.

Marchand was militant and confrontational. Within a year of his election as president in 1976, he led members out on what has been described by both union and management as a "bitter, violent" five-week strike in 1978. And in the early 1980s, while management was starry-eyed about the spectacular rise in oil prices, Marchand and his negotiating team managed to extract from Suncor a wage increase of 28 per cent over the two-year life of the contract. Management officials recall that oil prices were so high then that the company wasn't willing to risk foregoing so much as a single day of production. At the time the contract was signed, inflation was running at 10 per cent. Shortly afterward, it dropped to 5 per cent, and the contract fattened bank accounts and created great expectations among union members. That contract made Suncor's 1100 employees among the highest paid oil industry workers in the country.

The plant they worked in was the first major oil sands mine and refinery in Alberta. Built in the mid-1960s by Great Canadian Oil Sands Ltd. (GCOS), it opened in the fall of Canada's centennial, 1967. The principal partner in the consortium behind GCOS was Sun Oil. The plant, now owned and operated by the renamed Suncor, was designed to produce about 26 000 barrels of light, synthetic crude a day from a sea of tarry sand the size of New Brunswick that lies just below the muskeg of a huge area of northeastern Alberta.

When construction started on the GCOS plant, Neil Reimer, Canadian head of Oil, Chemical and Atomic Workers International (OCAW), attempted to organize the workers who were preparing the mine site. In his history of the ECWU, *Cracking the Canadian Formula: The Making of the Energy and Chemical Workers Union*, author Wayne Roberts says Reimer and the bullcook he had working inside signed up eighty of the one hundred and thirty workers on site and thought they had won certification. But the company responded by hiring another forty workers and diluting their majority. That was the opening shot of what was to be a twenty-one-year campaign by OCAW to gain a foothold in the oil sands industry.

GCOS and Sun Oil were determined to keep the union movement out of the plant. Reg Basken, current executive vice-president and secretary of the Communications, Energy and Paperworkers Union of Canada, says the company accomplished that by hiring workers at a company refinery in Sarnia and moving them to Fort McMurray to set up the Great Canadian Oil Sands Collective Bargaining Association, an in-house company union.

"They hired Edmonton lawyer Ammon Ackroyd to draft a constitution and take it to the labour board. Once they got the association set up and recognized as official bargaining agent, they promoted the Sarnia workers to supervisors. It was successful for twenty-one years in keeping us out of there," says Basken.

The archives of the OCAW tell the sorry story of the costly and relentless campaign the union waged to get a foot in the door at GCOS. In 1968, OCAW organizer Stu Sullivan was sent to Fort McMurray and was confronted by Mike Woodward, who threatened to beat the crap out of him. According to Roberts's account of the confrontation, Sullivan answered that a fistfight was the coward's way. "Why not listen to what I have to say?" Sullivan was convincing and he signed up Woodward, an armed forces boxing champ who later went on to form the Metis Association of Alberta. All that fall the two men worked together on the organizing campaign. They were defeated, in November, by a heartbreaking thirteen votes.

A year later, Sullivan was back with a campaign in which he stressed GCOS workers needed "an international union with professional bargainers who could stand up to an international company." Roberts says the workers' association responded with slick newspaper ads that boasted the association was "a selfish organization" that wasn't interested in playing second fiddle to the "needs of other units in an American union that locks all its units into cross-Canada bargaining."

Despite OCAW's failures, their organizing drives had a positive, cumulative effect. Stung by charges that it was a lapdog, in-house union, the leadership of the association began stressing to members that it was independent of the company. The change in attitude was profound enough that, in 1969, the association went out on strike for ten days. Created by the company as a blocking manoeuvre, the association began to transform itself into GCOS's worst nightmare: a militant and undisciplined union.

During that first strike in 1969, the picket lines went up not at the plant gate but thirty-six kilometres south at the approach to the GCOS-owned bridge crossing the Athabasca River. Allan Askeland, general manager of Diversified Transport, who has been on his company's busses taking management and scabs across the picket line in every dispute that has ever broken out at Suncor, says he remembers nudging the bus through the line in 1969 and having big Tiny O'Brien stand in front and refuse to move. Askeland says he just kept edging ahead, enduring Tiny's cursing. Some time after the dispute ended, Tiny took a job at Diversified and began working for Askeland. Fort McMurray is a small city, Askeland explains, and there is no percentage in hanging onto old grudges. Besides, he jokes, whenever he'd get exasperated with Tiny, he couldn't resist telling him that he should have run him over that day on the picket line.

From 1969 on, relations between the association and the company worsened. In 1971, after defeating yet another organizing drive by OCAW, the association hit the company with sixty-five lawsuits related to Suncor's housing rental policies. And a year later, the association leadership decided a name change was in order.

"We knew that the view of the Alberta labour movement was that associations like ours weren't real unions," recalls Gene Bacon, then a member of the association's executive.

"We also felt that our employer wasn't taking us seriously because we were just an association. So we struck a constitutional committee and renamed ourselves the McMurray Independent Oil Workers Union (MIOW). We became a duly certified union under the laws of Alberta."

Don Marchand became president after the name change, and within a year of assuming the presidency he led the members out on a five-week strike. It was a dispute over shift changes. The company was attempting to cut down on overtime and win back some control over shift assignments that it had given away in earlier years when it freely bought off association members in order to keep the OCAW at bay. MIOW was no pussycat, though, and the company discovered in that five-week dispute the depth of the distrust that now existed between workers and management.

Dan Comrie, who became president of the Suncor union in 1987, said by 1979 relations between the company and the union were so bad that when the company offered to bring all members into a dental plan for free, the members almost voted against it.

"Some people were saying, 'Yes, we can save dues.' Others were saying, 'They'll only get us in the plan and take it away from us. There's got to be a catch.' And the vote was very close," Comrie recalled.

By the end of the 1970s, Comrie said, with the price of oil rising rapidly, the company expanded the plant to increase production. It had been designed to produce 26 000 barrels a day. The changes allowed Suncor to produce more than 50 000 barrels a day.

"The wiring was outdated, the plant needed to be redone. General maintenance was never done. There were always emergencies. We were always putting out brush fires. It was good training though. You were working on stuff you'd never have to do anywhere else. The plant was dangerous. We had some serious fires, very serious fires. We were just lucky we had some good operators. The ones who had worked at Come By Chance (a Newfoundland refinery that was mothballed in 1976) were excellent."

The plant conditions and the isolation of McMurray meant that the attitude of many of the workers was "I'll get what I want or I'll leave," said Comrie.

"Suncor had lost control of the plant site. You worked the overtime you wanted. There was terrific turnover. I would guess between 25 and 35 per cent a year. I remember this unit leader in

21

the upgrader. I got a call from the shift supervisor. I went out and here's the unit leader sound asleep with his head on his desk. The shift supervisor goes over and shakes him once, shakes him twice. And the guy never even lifted his head. He said, 'Shake me again and I quit.' So the shift supervisor just wrote out the permit himself."

By then, the Suncor workforce had expanded and men and women with union experience from across the country had been hired. Cal Morrison was from Nova Scotia and had come through a twenty-nine-week strike as a Teamster. He hired on at Suncor in 1983 as a heavy equipment operator. Ed Stacey hailed from Port Blandford, Newfoundland and had been a unionized railroad man before taking a job at Suncor in 1980. Brian Campbell was born in Cornerbrook, Newfoundland, and had been in the Steelworkers Union, the Canadian Pulp and Paper Workers Union and the Machinist and Aerospace Workers Union before accepting a position as millwright with Suncor in 1981. Dave Scott was from the north of England and had been a unionized employee with Ontario Hydro before moving to Fort McMurray in 1981 to work for Suncor. Bill Johnston moved to Fort McMurray from Vancouver where he had been a member of an international union. There were hundreds more like them, men and women who had lived through strikes and wildcats and lockouts at railyards, refineries, plants and factories, and who knew about the benefits of union membership.

The presence of so many experienced union tradespeople convinced OCAW leaders that with perseverence, they could organize both Suncor and the new Syncrude plant. The previous failures had simply led to the conclusion that they needed a new approach. In 1978, OCAW sent Ian Thorn, a well-spoken refinery worker from Vancouver, to bang on doors and sell the benefits of membership in a large, international union like the OCAW. Thorn says he got inside most houses. "People wanted to talk. Some were anti-union but they wanted to talk about that too." Thorn later told his boss, Neil Reimer, that his most vivid impression of Fort McMurray in 1978 was that it seemed to be a small city powered by partying.

"The first time I went up there in 1978 they still had what they called Midsummer Night Madness, and that's when for about a week, around June 21, the longest day of the year, the streets were closed off, and it was just a party on the streets. It was daylight most of the night...It was just party all the time. When people weren't at work, they were partying. You could go into a bar and the bars were filled, like shoulder to shoulder. Somebody would say, 'Well, there's a party on at such and such a place.' So everybody just migrated to that address. It was a good opportunity to meet people, but you really couldn't do very much organizing when you went to one of these parties."

Thorn also found a high turnover at both the Suncor and Syncrude plants and many men, living without their families, who were working as much overtime as they could.

"The turnover at the two plants was something in the order of 25 to 30 per cent," Thorn told Reimer in an interview years later. "People were in and out; there was no feeling of, 'This is my community.' People were thinking, 'I'm here for a short period of time and then I'm gone.'"

When Thorn did manage to talk union with plant workers, the objection to signing up with OCAW that he heard over and over was that many workers were opposed to joining a union whose head office was in the US. They weren't keen to have a portion of their dues sent to Denver to support a large union bureaucracy. Marchand had done a great deal to convince his members that MIOW would suffer a dramatic loss of independence if it became a local of an international union.

That argument held until 1980 when OCAW split from its parent and became the Energy and Chemical Workers Union, based in Edmonton. Two years later, Reimer called Thorn and offered him a full-time job in Fort McMurray organizing the oil sands plants. Reimer told Thorn that he wanted him to "get involved in the social fabric of the community." Thorn accepted the challenge and moved to McMurray in January of 1983. Almost immediately he got himself onto the board of the United Way and began organizing a labour council. He had high visibility; the local media showered him with publicity.

Comrie said the MIOW executive was wary of Thorn's presence in the city.

"We just said that we were going to have to be very careful because they were here to steal our members. There's no doubt; at the time I think most of the executive board were committed to an independent union."

Comrie said there was real solidarity within MIOW. At the plant, "we had everybody. There was not a trade missing. There's not very many plants where you have miners, process operators, powerhouse operators all together in one union."

In 1979, revolution in Iran drove up the price of oil. The price rise made MIOW's leadership cocky and confident. Suncor was preparing in the early 1980s to embark on a major capital investment program at the plant and was willing to hike wages to keep labour peace. As Comrie put it, "First they wanted to get the plant into shape. Once they did that, they felt improved labour relations would come."

The cost of labour peace was a 27 per cent wage increase over a two-year contract. According to union members, Marchand's offer to the company was direct – put money on the table and MIOW would sign without any further discussion of other elements of the contract. The company agreed and put on the back burner all the outstanding contract disputes that had been grinding away at labour-management relations for years.

A year later, in 1983, Marchand, confident he had won a significant victory, decided to step down from the leadership of MIOW. Hans Hansen was voted in and he set about attempting to build a new relationship with the company. Hansen was conciliatory and constructive. Company officials apparently decided to take the opportunity to bring wages back into line with the remainder of the industry. The contract expired May 1, 1984 and by that spring, when negotiations began, the company was talking tough. Comrie says the company took Hansen's election as "a sign that the union might not want to fight so they gave us a wage freeze." As the May 1 expiry of the contract approached, the company negotiators began warning they would lock out MIOW. The company offered a zero per cent increase in the first year of the contract, 4 per cent in the second year and a 7.5 per cent cut in starting wages for new employees. Hansen countered that Suncor had made $103 million in profits in 1983 and was expected to make as much in 1984. He said he was encouraging his members to vote against the company's proposal. But the signs were ominous. Four hours before Suncor broke off talks and gave MIOW members formal notice of its lockout threat, the Alberta Labour Relations Board issued a troubling ruling. The board said companies that locked out their unionized employees could, after a mere twenty-five hours, legally terminate union contracts and begin hiring new employees at lower wages. Suncor spokesmen denied any connection between the ruling and the breakoff of talks. But the threat posed by both the ruling and Suncor's lockout warning hung in the air like the stench of sulphur. A tense week of mutual recriminations finally ended with several minor concessions on the part of management. MIOW members accepted both the freeze and the 4 per cent that had been offered. But there was bitterness. Members felt Suncor had been gunning for them and that a battle was looming. Many said afterward they felt Suncor was out to break the union. That talk was to persist.

By early 1985, relations at the Suncor plant had deteriorated into a state of siege. A staggering 357 grievances were filed during the year, absenteeism rates soared and MIOW members were calling in sick in record numbers. Accidents on the job were increasing. Chafing with exasperation on the sidelines, Marchand decided to run for the presidency again. He was opposed by Eric Schmidt, a unit leader in extraction and one of the first operators hired at the plant. As the election campaign ran its course that fall, MIOW members split into two factions. Comrie said one group "wanted Marchand back to beat the shit out of the company and the others wanted Schmidt. They said, 'Hey, here's a leader, an excellent operator, we respect him, can work with him, and he would do a hell of a job and maybe the relationship would improve.'"

The vote resulted, incredibly, in a tie. A second vote was scheduled two weeks later, and Marchand won that one by a slim majority.

"Don just did his work and got his people out," says Comrie.

"As soon as he was elected the company started saying Marchand is not going to run the plant. They (Suncor) must have gone up to six full-time labour relations people. They needed that many to respond to our grievances, to write back that there was no violation of the collective agreement. There was no intent to settle any of the differences. The relationship was so bad that something was going to take place."

Almost as soon as Marchand reassumed the presidency, Suncor assigned Ron Wood to head the human relations department. Tough, experienced and well-known in Fort McMurray, Wood had moved to the city in 1969. He started with Suncor as a buyer in purchasing and had, over the years, managed almost every area of the plant and had eventually become senior manager of the entire facility. He headed the company's negotiating team in 1984 and was given overall responsibility for the human relations department a year later. Comrie says "Wood was a good guy until they moved him into human relations. He could deliver a mandate. A tough guy."

Wood himself says he first met Marchand years earlier and that they got along. Both their boys played hockey and Wood even coached Marchand's son at one point. Wood says when he was manager of the materials department he "never had a grievance and that was primarily because we had good supervisors." Still, Wood was realistic about what was coming and he wasn't a man to shirk from shouldering a hard task. Wood says during the years when oil prices were rising, "we didn't want to have strikes. You could say we were bullied into it (handsome wage increases and other contract concession), but we were selfishly cruising that way anyway."

Then, when prices started falling in late 1985, "MIOW just didn't want to acknowledge some of the realities, and of course that frustrated management, and both parties dug in their heels. Both became rigid. And without flexibility you don't resolve issues," says Wood.

Suncor had made a major capital investment in the plant in 1982, and once that was completed, the company began to tackle labour relations problems. The first step, says Wood, was investing in better supervision.

"We focused in on training of supervisors to become better management and supervisory people and our expectations were higher and we began doing performance appraisals on supervisors. We set goals and objectives and monitored and reviewed them weekly, monthly, quarterly and annually."

Wood said management understood that if they had good, well-trained supervisors, then the payoff would come in fewer grievances.

"But if you have a union that is totally antagonistic toward supervisors, and you go into a grievances process, you are not going to get resolution. Sometimes the union was rigid and sometimes management was rigid."

In 1985, Suncor hired a consulting company, "to come in and give advice on cost reductions," said Gene Bacon. "It was some sort of efficiency consulting company. They were undertaking what is known in the industry as a slash and burn exercise. You carve out significant chunks of the organization. It is the type of exercise that focuses on the value of work and whether it is required. It is a very stressful exercise. I was working in the heavy equipment maintenance facility at the time (doing budget analysis). The consulting people came through, did some preliminary work and said 'You have a minimum 15 per cent too many people.' They said we could cut 150 to 160 people."

Looking back now, Bacon is critical of the decision to hire the consulting firm.

"When those people were in an area going through their studies it was evident to everybody in an area what was happening. They were studying the motions of people on the floor. And that was contentious. They did very little to ask people for methods, for their views. At first I took them to be a tool the company hired to help me find ways of running my part of the business better. As it unfolded it became fairly evident that that wasn't the case, that they were there to reduce manpower, period. They had their own methods for going through the exercise. In retrospect it accomplished very little because it did not address the work component of the business. It only addressed the resource component. It didn't even examine whether work was required. It added up the work that was there and said, 'Ok, that takes five people instead of six.' In the final analysis it was fairly arbitrary."

But at the time, Suncor management used the consulting company's recommendations as a roadmap to guide them back to profitability. When oil prices were high, Suncor needed to show the plant could be a consistent producer and it needed the revenue stream from the oil production.

"To shut down 50 000 barrels a day when oil prices were $40 a barrel, that's a lot of money," says Wood. But when prices started sliding down toward costs, management had no choice but to consider how costs could be reduced, says Wood.

"We needed flexibility of movement of people. The lack of flexibility forced us into paying a lot of overtime. We were paying double time for overtime and then if that ran into a statutory holiday then it was four times. There was no question that people were manipulating that. Phoning in sick so friends could get overtime. Lots of games were being played. Or a guy coming on shift would refuse overtime so somebody else on days off would have to be called in. That person would get double and a call-out fee as well. It was costing a horrendous amount of money. The company began taking a forceful position in 1984. We told the union negotiating committee 'Better take the offer on the table and sell it to the membership because it isn't going to get any better. That was the opening of the dam from management's point of view. Those negotiations were tough. Hans Hansen was president then and, of course, what made it so much more difficult for him was that the 1982 negotiations had been so successful for the union. Marchand had gotten all those big bucks. So in 1984 the negotiations were tough. We managed to get better control of overtime. We got the chit system. Under that system, a week before your days off you would put in your chit to volunteer for overtime for the positions that you were qualified for. The chit system gave supervisors a list of fellas up front that they could call to distribute the overtime. There was an equalization of overtime."

For Suncor managers, the 1984 negotiations only whetted their appetite. There were more cuts they wanted to make, more concessions they had made in previous years that they wanted to take back. And so in the fall of 1985, with the contract due to expire on April 30, 1986, they began planning for a lockout.

"Our plan was we were either going to have a collective agreement in place on May 1 or we were going to have a lockout. If we were going to have a dispute then we were going to manage it and the only tool we had to manage it was to lock out MIOW members," says Wood.

By initiating the dispute on May 1, the company then had all summer to let it play out. The dispute had, without question, to be resolved by freeze-up in the fall. To have it extend past freeze-up meant attempting to run the plant in winter without experienced MIOW operators. And that would be asking for trouble. If the plant went down during winter, for whatever reason, it would take operators with consummate skill and experience in running a plant that far north to bring it back up. Without those people, the plant could be down all winter.

With that timing in mind, all that fall of 1985, management was busy contacting other Sun Oil refineries, lining up the necessary tradespeople to run the plant and continue producing oil after May 1. You may be needed for the entire spring and summer, many of them were told.

I'd rather be strongly wrong than weakly right.

TALLULAH BANKHEAD

Some people thought the lockout was an attempt to crush the union. They considered themselves peaceful men and women who had done nothing to justify such a massive show of intimidating force.

OVERLEAF: The lockout had serious consequences, but, as one Newfoundland dad told his son upon hearing of his arrest, "If you'd done anything different, I'd have been disappointed." John Trottman is put into handcuffs.

CHAPTER THREE

BUYOUT
HOLDOUT
LOCKOUT

THREE WEEKS into 1986, with contract negotiations about to begin, Suncor management called a meeting with MIOW's bargaining committee and told them 280 people would be cut from the payroll at the plant. Mike Supple, oil sands group vice president, told the unionists and, later, the media that generous early retirement packages would be offered as well as buyouts for younger employees who wanted to return to school. In addition, there would be relocation allowances and retraining programs on offer.

Marchand and his colleagues were impressed with the generosity of the buyout packages, but they balked at Supple's request that they sign an agreement waiving some of the conditions of the existing contract to allow the company to transfer employees to lower paying jobs if the voluntary resignation program didn't attract enough recruits. After discussing the plan with Supple,

Marchand and his colleagues said, in a statement they later sent to local newspapers, that they agreed to do their "part and cooperate with the company on the job transfers (rollbacks) if the voluntary resignation program did not produce enough results."

When Supple met reporters that same day he made every effort to assure employees and residents of Fort McMurray that the program was voluntary. Still, the announcement came as a shock. A no-layoff policy had been in effect at the plant since its opening, and regardless of how carefully Supple chose his words, he was signaling the end of an era. He pointed out that oil prices had fallen from $42.26 a barrel in December 1984 to $34.05 at the time of the announcement. And oil prices, he pointed out, were still rolling downhill.

Despite Marchand's agreement that he would cooperate with the program, when asked by reporters to comment, he attacked Suncor. He told reporters that Suncor had "led the people of Fort McMurray down the garden path." He said the company had received more than $300 million in tax concessions from the federal and provincial governments in exchange for a commitment to add 175 new union jobs. He said the union had grown by a grand total of twenty. Supple countered by saying Suncor had created 400 new jobs since 1976.

The war of words notwithstanding, the almost immediate effect of Suncor's offer was a rush for the exits. MIOW members all across the plant raced to tell the company they wanted the buyout or early retirement. A day after the company announcement Marchand was telling the press that it appeared the company "will have no problem filling up their quota of 280...People are not happy with the way they've been treated. They're fed up with the way the company's been pushing them around."

The voluntary layoff plan had sprung directly from the consulting company's recommendations for deep cuts in the labour force.

Bacon agreed that the company had plenty of "takers on enhanced early retirements because it was pretty attractive for anyone fifty-five plus."

Formal contract talks between management and MIOW began a month later, on February 3. The day before they began, the company's in-house newspaper, *The Oilsander*, carried a front page story that showed oil prices had plummeted from over $36 in December 1985 to under $24 by February, a drop of more than $10 in two months. Given the losses the falling price of oil meant for the oil sands plant, company officials were in no mood for tender talk.

On the first day of negotiations, both Suncor and MIOW returned to the issue of the voluntary layoff program. By then the company was rethinking the program, given both the numbers of employees volunteering to leave and that the union was testy about how the program was being applied. A series of fractious meetings followed throughout February and the first part of March. Then, suddenly, on March 10, Supple informed the union that the company was withdrawing the voluntary job reduction program. It would be replaced, he said, by internal transfers and outright layoffs. The number of jobs to be cut would also increase from 280 to 350.

Shortly after Supple's announcement, thirty-seven workers were laid off. All of them were given layoff notices after they had refused a transfer to positions which paid, in some cases, up to $4.33 an hour less than their old jobs.

The announcement and the layoffs antagonized to the extreme the MIOW negotiating team and left the union's members confused and edgy. The company had given with one hand and was now taking away with the other. It seemed terribly arbitrary. If you had been quick off the mark in applying for the original package, you got a handsome settlement to leave. If you were not so quick, you got transferred to a lower-paying job or were simply laid off. That got the blood stirring among MIOW members. It didn't seem fair, they told each other.

Adding oil to the flames, one of the people laid off was the wife of MIOW negotiating team member Gary Morrison.

"She worked at top shop," MIOW negotiator Dan Comrie recalls. "They just called her up one day and said 'we are letting you go.' This happened while we were negotiating. I'm still convinced it was related."

And Comrie wasn't the only one who was suspicious. Dave Scott, an energetic, forceful member of the MIOW negotiating team, is still convinced that "they let her go because of Gary. I think there were tactics played by different people throughout the organization. In Gary's case, they thought it would split the negotiating committee. They were willing to play games with people's minds and careers."

Marchand and his colleagues on the MIOW executive immediately challenged the company over the reading of the layoff language.

Bacon said the language dispute centred on "what category of folks you have to roll into the picture before you start applying seniority. The company took the view that apprentices are a separate category from a trade. We had laid off some apprentices who had fourteen or fifteen years of service and some mechanics with only a year. That became a major bone of contention."

Dave Scott said the consulting company's recommendations had set the table for the discussions. MIOW members in general and the negotiating team in particular were ready to believe the worst. Then the dispute over the layoffs brought everything to a head.

"What made everybody so upset was that the company was setting out to violate the most sacred provisions of the contract – seniority provisions," said Scott.

On top of that, the company had offered the members some options, said Scott, and then had swiftly taken them away. Union members knew they weren't in a strong bargaining position, what with oil prices dropping, but they felt they were being sucker punched by a bully, and that sooner or later they'd have to start punching back.

Marchand's formal response to the proposed transfers and layoffs was to file a grievance. He argued that the layoffs violated the collective agreement. Workers with the least seniority must be laid off first, he said, but Suncor wasn't following this practice.

"We've had guys with ten, eleven and twelve years of seniority laid off. And there are other men with six months to a year's experience who're staying on."

To illustrate the unfairness of what the company was doing, MIOW invited the press to interview Wilf Blanchette, a father of seven children, who was laid off after he refused a transfer to a lower-paying job. The soft-spoken forty-seven-year-old said he had been working at Suncor for thirty months before getting his lay-off notice. He explained he had refused the transfer because he supported the union's position.

"I could have survived on $12-and-change an hour but most of these guys would have trouble. If it were up to me alone I would have taken the transfer, but this is a union and we support each other."

Blanchette added that the apprentices with fourteen years of service who were laid off were being penalized "because they tried to better themselves." They had joined the apprentice training program and then been snagged by the layoff policy, he said.

Perhaps the most poignant note of his remarks was his comment that his vacation pay was the only termination benefit he would receive.

By late March, Suncor had made a formal contract offer to MIOW, an offer that the union executive considered an insult. Evidently fearing that the union would not fairly represent the offer to its members, Wood summarized the offer in a letter that was sent out to all employees. Given the circumstances as he drafted the letter – the papers were carrying news that the spot price for the benchmark US crude oil had dropped to a nine-year low of $9.90 on the New York Mercantile Exchange – Wood likely believed that he could convince employees that he was offering them the best deal possible.

"We believe our position recognizes today's economic realities and demonstrates our sincere effort to enter into a fair collective agreement," Wood wrote in his preamble. The offer itself included: no initial wage increase but a 3 per cent increase if oil prices rose to $25 or higher; an obligation by workers to accept the pay offered in positions they might be transferred to; a reduction of overtime pay to time-and-a-half from double time; and a provision that would oblige employees to pay for part of their bussing costs.

Marchand organized two meetings, on March 31 and April 1, to discuss the offer with the membership. During those meetings he said that the union understood the difficult position the company had been placed in by the fall of the price of oil. He said he and his fellow negotiating team members had told Suncor that they would accept the layoffs if the job reduction package the company had originally offered were reinstated. After his presentation, more than 90 per cent of those present voted, by a show of hands, to reject Suncor's offer.

After the second meeting, on April 1, the members' rejection of the contract was answered by the start of the layoffs. The company hadn't planned it that way, it just so happened that the layoffs were to take effect on April Fools' Day. It couldn't have been more unfortunate or more provocative timing.

Bacon said there was nothing sinister or threatening about it, just that the "layoffs occurred that day and it was part of that puzzle and part of cost reduction. We reduced our maintenance staff in heavy equipment by, I think, thirteen and then in our overburden operation I think we cut about thirty out of that as well. This was strictly layoffs. At that time oil prices had dropped like a stone. We were sufficiently ahead in overburden so we could slow that down and cutting thirty-five to forty people was pure cash saving."

Two day later Suncor added insult to injury by suspending contract negotiations and, once again, warning that they would lock out MIOW members May 1 if a contract wasn't signed by then. Company officials said they had broken off negotiations because the union had refused to conduct a government-supervised ballot of the contract offer. They insisted that a show-of-hands vote wasn't good enough.

Marchand was incredulous.

"I've never heard of such a thing as government supervision for a contract vote," he said during a newspaper interview. "I told Ron Wood there is no way we'll accept that."

Company spokesman Doug Hodge agreed it was unusual but said, "these are uncommon times."

Marchand responded by submitting a request to the Labour Relations Board for a government-supervised strike vote.

By now it was abundantly clear to many within MIOW that a full-blown labour dispute was in the offing. The more prudent

and experienced union members began making formal preparations.

Larry Colclough, an equipment operator from Ontario who
had hired on at Suncor in 1978, said he and his wife Peggy had
bought a house in the fall of 1985.

"What with payments and three kids we had no extra money
kicking around. By March, I knew we were going to be locked out
or on strike so I went in to see Betty Agnew, the loan manager at
the Bank of Montreal," Larry recalls.

"We opened up my file and I said, 'I can't afford this come
May 1.' She said, 'What are we going to do?' I said, 'That's what
I'm here to discuss.' I said, 'I've got a good paying job with good
benefits and I don't want to lose that job or this house.' So Betty
told me, 'Don't talk so foolish. Come to me on May 1 if there is a
lockout.' And that visit made all the difference later."

Dave Scott, who could see from his vantage point on the
negotiating team that relations were headed for a fight, began
putting money aside as early as 1984. Still, he feared that if it came
to a lockout, he'd be in a pickle. His wife was an engineer at Suncor
who would have to cross the MIOW picket line or be terminated.

"I thought it would be emotionally tearing."

Others were trapped by simply bad timing or by their own
optimism.

Brian Campbell, a millwright from Newfoundland who had
become a shop steward shortly after his arrival at Suncor, bought
a new car in March, was carrying a big mortgage and, with his
wife, Yvonne, had two kids still in diapers.

"We didn't prepare too well. But anything is possible. I thought
anything could happen."

Brian McFalls, who worked as an operator in the powerhouse, said his children were six and eight in the spring of 1986
and his wife was working as a school bus driver. They too didn't
make any special preparations.

"We weren't too horribly worried about it because we were
kinda thinking it would last maybe a month. I sure never thought
it was going to last six months."

Ray and Pamela Lays, both originally from Nova Scotia, had

four kids by 1986 and "were renting an apartment and didn't have much money saved," says Pamela.

"We knew something was coming, something was gonna happen," Ray adds.

Their only preparation for the dispute emerged during a conversation Pamela had with her parents. Her father worked at Syncrude and was a devoted supporter of unions.

"My parents just said when Ray's not working, move in with us."

Kerry Wood was perhaps in the most unique and awkward position. The daughter of Suncor's lead negotiator, Ron Wood, Kerry was a MIOW member who had been working in the plant warehouse since 1980. In 1986, she was also living with Suncor security guard Jed Matthews.

"I was on maternity leave in March and my UIC maternity benefits were due to run out on May 7," she says.

"My dad and I never talked about it," says Kerry, and she and Jed had difficulty discussing it as well.

Meanwhile, the union was taking the necessary steps for a strike or a lockout.

Bill Ross, a former hard rock miner from Manitoba, was safety coordinator and a shop steward. He was drawn into quiet preparations.

"We started organizing committees, selecting picket captains, organizing staff for the hall, planning a food store."

Of all the union's preparations the most significant was the approach made to its old foe, the Energy and Chemical Workers Union. After years of beating off organizing drives and raids, MIOW was ready to seek the expertise and financial strength of the ECWU.

In October 1985, just after his return to the presidency and well before the start of negotiations with Suncor, Marchand met with ECWU's Ian Thorn, who was now head of the Fort McMurray Labour Council as well as key player in the United Way.

"Don made the point clear that he knew where they were going with Suncor and that he would deliver the membership of MIOW to ECWU," said Thorn. "Don said, 'Leave it to me.' In other words, he wanted me to stay in the background and not come out formally calling for the affiliation. At first I was not certain. But very shortly I was sure that Don was sincere."

If Thorn was sceptical, he had good reason to be. According to Thorn's boss Neil Reimer, Marchand had turned up at the ECWU offices one day in the early 1980s and had asked about the possibility of an affiliation between ECWU and MIOW.

"So we sat down several days and negotiated it...He had promised me that he was going to bring it before his Board of Directors and all that," Reimer recalled.

But Dan Comrie, who was then on the MIOW executive, said Marchand never did bring the deal back to his board.

"The board sent him...to pursue an affiliation with ECW. He (Marchand) came back and reported that it was not feasible and that was the end of the subject," Comrie told Reimer during an interview for a history of the OCAW and ECWU.

Reimer said he believes the negotiations fell through because he refused Marchand's suggestion that he be allowed "to retire at full wages for the rest of his life."

Now, however, Marchand had his back to the wall. Suncor was playing hardball and MIOW had about $200,000 in its strike fund. With 1100 members, he knew the money wouldn't sustain MIOW for long in a work stoppage. And so back he went to ECWU.

Marchand explains his actions thusly: "All I can say is that I do believe they (Suncor) were out to break the contract. So I talked to a few people about joining the ECWU. I had opposed this in the past. I felt we were better off by ourselves. Right up until the crunch. A good union can look after itself."

Comrie remembers the worrying discussions he had with Marchand before and after Don talked to Thorn.

"Don and I had no illusions about what was going to happen. We knew we needed money. We had maybe $200,000. But a strike in a northern town, people don't have a network of relatives they can rely on. No place to go and eat dinner. Nobody phoning you saying, 'Come on over. I know you are on strike. Have dinner at our place.' Up there we knew that anybody phoning would be on strike too.

"We also needed the expertise of the ECWU. I wanted help at the table. I think Don's interest was the money. But I wanted expertise at the bargaining table. We couldn't talk to anybody. We couldn't get to the top people at Suncor. The easiest thing is to get on the bricks. The hardest is to get off. To get off you need people in the union who can get to the top company people and talk."

Comrie believed the situation was bleak and desperate.

"I believe Suncor was frustrated and tired and they had started to look at the best thing, which was breaking the union. I think that had we stayed an independent, they would have achieved that."

By February, Comrie says he and Marchand were making weekly trips to Thorn's office to talk.

"We knew they (ECWU) would either sign us or raid us. If you talked to some of the old-timers, they talked about booting their asses (ECWU people) and telling them to get out of town. Ian (Thorn) knew what was going on."

Marchand wanted to deal with bigger players than Thorn so at some point after Christmas 1985, Kerry Woollard of the Canadian Labour Congress's (CLC) Edmonton office was drawn into the discussions. ECWU was a member of the CLC and Woollard acted, says Thorn, as "a facilitator, a moderator, a mediator. Don wanted to talk to people at the top. He was looking for the best deal he could get. So Don talked to me and Reg (Basken, executive vice president of the ECWU) through Kerry. Kerry was very good in the role he played. He was very professional. Don made it clear he wanted a job and that was definitely not in the cards as far as Reg was concerned."

In April, Basken entered the picture.

Comrie says he, Marchand, Thorn and Basken met "in a hotel room. Reg put out the offer. An affiliation for two years. Access to strike money. They would help with negotiations and with training and education. After two years we could vote on whether to merge with ECWU. Couldn't have asked for a better deal. But Don was nervous. He didn't want to lose the power, the control. As an independent, MIOW was collecting two hours pay from each member in dues every month. If we joined ECWU, an hour would stay with us and an hour's dues would go to the national. The local was paying Don's wages. But the affiliation agreement interested him because he could see that we could always get out of it."

Basken says Marchand, in what can only be described as brinkmanship, agreed to the affiliation but "specifically asked to be kept out of the strike fund. He said they didn't want to contribute to it. We didn't get a penny from them."

An agreement was struck, and Basken recalls having to write into it the fact that MIOW would not have to contribute to the strike fund and would not be allowed to draw from it. Marchand was evidently hoping to use the affiliation, an agreement that afforded him a backdoor escape hatch, to bluff Suncor. He apparently believed that Suncor might back down from its threatening bargaining position if it knew that MIOW had the might of a national and wealthy labour union affiliated with the Canadian Labour Congress standing alongside him. He saw the affiliation as a bargaining chip, one that could be discarded after it had served its purpose.

After the agreement had been struck, Marchand presented it to the membership for a vote. It was endorsed by a 90 per cent majority. The day after the vote, on April 9, news of the affiliation made it into the local newspaper. The story noted that MIOW had established a link to the ECWU and the CLC. But Marchand hadn't even mentioned the ECWU in his interview with the newspaper. He said that the CLC's information and training resources would be of advantage to the local organizations and "all unions should help each other out." When asked, he denied that the affiliation had anything to do with the deadlock in contract negotiations with Suncor, although he admitted that "a lot of things might happen" with the CLC affiliation.

Kerry Woollard was also at the meeting and talked to the press as well. He was quoted as saying that the CLC's resources might be brought to bear on the negotiating process by providing MIOW executives with training in the collective bargaining process.

"We are available for their purposes," Woollard said. "And we could sit down at the table with the MIOW team and Suncor during further discussions. It would be unusual but not impossible."

What nobody mentioned in the story, what nobody talked about, was the ECWU's strike fund. Marchand may have believed he could fool Suncor into thinking he had won himself the financing for a strike of any length. But Basken doesn't believe the company was fooled for a moment.

"They probably knew we weren't giving MIOW access to the strike fund," Basken says. "The company probably knew that. So they probably felt good about locking them out because MIOW had an affiliation but no right to our strike fund."

A week after the story of the affiliation appeared, MIOW members met, and in government-supervised balloting, 91.7 per cent of them voted in favour of a strike. Marchand had his mandate. Now, he offered an olive branch. A strike would be a last resort, he said.

"We've already offered to get back to the table but their committee refused. All we can do now is wait for the call."

The call, when it came, was a request by the company for the services of a provincially-appointed mediator. With exactly a week left before the company's lockout was set to begin, both sides met with mediator Dale Simpson at the Peter Pond Hotel on April 23. Neither side wished to say anything to the press about the mediation talks. Simpson's only public remarks were that the talks were ongoing and that there was no deadline.

Roberts, in his book *Cracking the Canadian Formula*, says Marchand's final offer to the company was to leave the agreement as it was and negotiate raises if and when the price of oil climbed out of the basement. According to Roberts, Marchand was told by a company official, "You're too fucking late."

It's not clear who made that remark but Ron Wood says by that stage in the talks, after thirty-nine frustrating negotiating meetings with MIOW, management had "every i dotted and every t crossed. We were absolutely confident we could run the plant during a lockout. Everything was riding on it. We had had to sell it to our president and he had had to sell it to Sun Oil. We were very confident. We knew what we wanted and what we needed. And we couldn't make any progress. We couldn't get the union to negotiate."

When the mediation talks began, Wood and his team had put in place all the elements needed to do battle with MIOW. Nothing but major concessions could have avoided the lockout at that point. Wood says MIOW's affiliation agreement with the ECWU and CLC didn't change anything. He says he was actually looking forward to dealing with the ECWU.

"I thought it would be a lot easier dealing with ECWU than dealing with people who give you the impression sometimes that they don't know what they are doing and are inconsistent. Dealing with ECWU you knew where they were coming from and you knew it before it happened because of their open dialogue. We could never get that established with MIOW."

Not surprisingly, mediation talks broke down two days after they started. Layoff procedures and overtime pay were the two major stumbling blocks, Marchand told reporters.

Now events accelerated like a runaway train. If union members were glum about the breakdown of talks, they were made fearful as well by a story that appeared in that day's edition of *The Edmonton Journal*. Phones across the city hummed that night with word of the article, which ran under the weight of the headline: "Suncor Ponders McMurray Plant Closure."

The article attributed to Suncor chairman Bill Loar the remark that the company was seriously considering shutting down its money-losing oil sands plant if world oil prices remained depressed for long. The article also quoted company president Tom Thompson, who talked to reporters after the company's annual meeting in Toronto. Thompson was more equivocal. He said, the article noted, that Suncor had been actively considering closing the plant, which was then losing about $6 for every barrel it produced. Asked when a decision would be made, Thompson said the company was still convinced that low oil prices were just a short-term problem.

"If you think the plant has long term viability, then you tough it out; if you think it hasn't, then you should move to close it down. We can tough it out for a while."

It is difficult to imagine that those remarks were unintentional given the battle that was looming in Fort McMurray. Were they intended to shake apart the resolve of the union members? In Fort McMurray, the local press scrambled to put that question and others to Thompson. The remarks were incendiary. Staff reporters at *Fort McMurray Today* reached Thompson, who denied that Suncor was seriously considering closing its plant. But then, in the next breath, he brought the possibility back to life.

"Suncor has been in Fort McMurray a long time and they've been through tough times before, and they'll make it through tough times again. We have no intention of closing at this stage."

At this stage. It was subtle and it was effective. What Thompson did with that phrase was to shift the psychological burden of responsibility for the future of the plant onto the shoulders of MIOW members. At this stage. Suncor knew the situation was serious, Thompson was saying, but did MIOW members know? It was a last minute attempt to drive the nervous to rebellion.

For the most part, Thompson's remarks were greeted with derision. Many MIOW members saw it as fearmongering, as blackmail. Marchand and his lieutenants worked feverishly to convince the membership that Suncor was bluffing, that the timing of the remarks explained all. Still, the threat lingered and never faded. It would always be there, would surface again and again during the course of the dispute. It was a weapon and it would be used by local businessmen, by MIOW dissidents, by politicians and many others to challenge the wisdom and authority of MIOW leaders.

As a tactical manoeuvre, it was brilliantly played, and it demonstrated clearly that Suncor was girded for battle. Now Marchand knew, if he had ever before had any doubts, that there was no more room or more time for bluffing. Suncor was lining up MIOW for a beating. Marchand had miscalculated. All that stood between his members and a good drubbing was a $200,000 strike fund. Desperate for last minute help, on April 30, hours before the lockout was to begin, Marchand asked Thorn to help him track down Basken. They contacted him in Geneva, where the ECWU leader was attending a conference.

"We are about to be locked out and we need access to the strike fund," Basken remembers Marchand telling him, via Thorn, over the intercontinental phone line.

"I said, 'Well, we are going to have to change the agreement because you aren't in the strike fund.'"

Basken says he thought about it and decided to gamble.

"I said, 'Ok, we will pay you strike benefits.' And I took quite a risk. I had quite a fight with my executive because we ended up paying strike benefits for four weeks before the board even approved it. And MIOW hadn't paid one penny to ECWU and here we were paying 1000 people strike benefits. This happened within hours of the lockout."

You should never have your best trousers on when you turn out to fight for freedom and truth.

HENRIK IBSEN

The plant, the picketers could see, was still running. They knew that the camp inside was filled with operators and engineers brought in from across the country to keep the refinery pumping oil.
(From l to r) Rick Cooke, Keith Leamon.

OVERLEAF: The lockout began at midnight on May 1, 1986. Those whose shift ended at midnight left the plant and joined the picket line.

CHAPTER FOUR

TOE TO THE LINE

JUST AFTER MIDNIGHT on May 1, MIOW members whose shift had just ended, and who had driven to work, parked near Highway 63 and joined the line of cheering picketers that was forming. The cold night air crackled with tension.

Suncor owns the access road that leads to the plant from Highway 63, but the first forty-six metres between the highway and the access road is public property. In that forty-six metre area, the picketers built fires and staked-out a site where they would park a trailer the next morning.

Suncor's property line was marked by a fence and gate. Behind it stood a security trailer. As the number of picketers increased, several moved to shut the gate but Marchand talked them out of it.

"It's their job now (running the plant), let them do it," he told hooting and cheering members. He also cautioned his fellow unionists to stay off company property.

In the shadows behind the fence, the picketers could see

security guards with walkie-talkies, a truck with a public-address system mounted on it and spotlights mounted on poles five metres high.

Despite the cold and the dark there was mounting anger on the line. The plant, the picketers could see, was still running. They knew that the camp inside was filled with operators and engineers brought in from across the country to keep the refinery pumping oil. Rumours had swept the union ranks that Suncor was going to lock them out for twenty-five hours and then begin offering people jobs at much lower rates. Even if that didn't prove to be the case, there was still talk of Suncor's threat to mothball the facility. The company wanted major concessions and had locked them out to obtain them. Was Suncor determined to break the union in the process? The rumours on the line that night mutated into the darkest conspiracies, and by early morning light the picketers were grim with determination. If the company wanted a fight, they felt, then they were going to defend themselves.

Three days before the line formed at the plant, Suncor had formally served MIOW with notice of the lockout, which was to begin at 12:01 a.m., May 1. MIOW had responded by informing the company that it would strike on May 1. Some members of the union felt that the strike notice was a precautionary move that would prevent Suncor from simply locking them out for twenty-five hours and hiring a new workforce. Whatever the case, when the Alberta Labour Relations Board was asked to define the conflict, it chose to label the dispute a strike/lockout.

As the sun rose that morning, the first skirmishes broke out. There to record every incident was a professional photographer hired by Suncor.

Allan Askeland, general manager of Diversified Transport, was in the front seat of the first bus to approach the picket line. Diversified had, and still has, the contract to bus Suncor employees from their homes to the plant, and Askeland says his company was contractually obligated to continue the service regardless of the picket line. The Suncor employees on that bus, as well as those on three other busses parked out on the highway waiting for the lead vehicle to cross, were mostly female clerical staff.

In the affidavit Askeland swore out four days later, he said that the bus turned off Highway 63 toward the plant at 7:45 a.m. on May 1 and was immediately stopped by picketers. Askeland said they crowded around the front of the bus, ripping off a windshield wiper, banging on the windows.

While Askeland tried to keep everybody on the bus calm, he saw Marchand knock on the window and motion for him to open the door. Askeland refused to open up. Marchand, Askeland said, then began banging on the door and, suddenly, the bus began to rock side to side. With each rocking motion, the fear inside reached heart-stopping pitch.

MIOW member Brian Campbell was on the line at midnight, but went home for a couple of hours sleep before returning the next morning.

"I was there first thing the next morning when that first bus arrived. That bus was really rocking. It was close to getting out of hand. Somebody could have really gotten hurt."

Then, Askeland said in his affidavit, without warning, somebody in a white toque threw a rock at the driver's side of the windshield and it cracked the glass.

"The rock didn't come through," Askeland said in an interview years later, "But it scared everybody."

Campbell said he was facing the bus when "a rock came from behind me and smashed the windshield. It must have been a big one. I was momentarily stunned."

Dave Scott, a member of the MIOW bargaining committee and one of the union's troubleshooters frequently called out to the line, believes that the rock was thrown for a good reason.

"The driver of the first bus was asked to stop but he didn't. He just kept on going very slowly. Inside that bus were a lot of cameras. That driver was told to edge his way into the crowd," Scott insists.

"Then one guy in front lost his footing. Because guys were pushing, and as he lost his footing he grabbed the windshield wiper to stop from falling. People behind him got frightened, and the only way they knew to stop that bus was to put a rock through the windshield. And that's all it needed."

Now, Askeland gave the driver the order to ease back and head north to a place where the bus could turn around for the trip back to Fort McMurray. But he wasn't out of the woods yet.

After the bus had turned and was headed south, a brown Ford station wagon overtook them and, as it passed the bus, someone on the passenger's side threw something that smacked the bus on the side, startling the driver.

Campbell says by now everyone on the line was jacked for a fight.

"There was lots of whooping and hollering. The mood was up."

Later that day there were more skirmishes. By early afternoon, the picketers were littering the road with tires, logs and lumber to ensure that all vehicles would stop at the line. At 2:30 p.m., another Diversified bus pulled up and was greeted by 150 picketers.

"Rock concerts" caused thousands of dollars of damage to busses crossing the line. One mother caught up in the moment recalls she "threw a rock and smashed a window, but I never got caught because I was so short the cops couldn't see me. It made me angry. Here, I didn't have enough money to take my daughter for an ice cream."

They massed onto the road. A security guard used the public address system to ask the picketers to move off the road. The request was greeted with stony indifference.

Now it was the turn of the janitors. They came in two vans, and attempted twice to turn onto the access road leading to the plant. Both times they were rebuffed while a security guard again ordered the picketers to move off the road. All the while, the guards and the professional photographer were firing off rolls of film, capturing every precious moment for posterity.

Daniela Basile, owner of the janitorial company, later said in his affidavit that the picketers pounded on his van and shouted at him:"Nobody's getting through this picket line." Explaining to a picketer that he was just attempting to fulfil his contract, Basile said he was told by another MIOW member:"You've done your part. Now go home."

The final drama of the day was played out at 9:00 p.m. that night. An ambulance driven by a security guard approached the picket line and was stopped. Earlier in the day, the head security guard on duty had told Marchand that an ambulance was coming out of the plant with an injured worker. Marchand had the picketers immediately clear a path for the ambulance, which raced off to Fort McMurray. But that night when the ambulance returned, it was stopped and the picketers asked what was in the back. When they were told that it was a patient who had been treated at Fort McMurray, six picketers started rocking the car. They insisted that the back be opened so they could verify who was in it. The nurse in the back told the driver not to open the door so the driver suggested the picketers look in the back window. But that wasn't acceptable to them and they tried all the door handles. A standoff ensued until two security guards were brought over to stand at the back of the ambulance to protect the patient. Then the door was opened, the inside inspected and the ambulance let through the line. All of this was recorded and submitted in an affidavit.

By then, the photographer, the security guards, the Diversified employees, the janitors and the secretaries had done their part. Suncor now had the evidence it needed for the injunction, which the company appealed to the courts for the following day.

Dave Scott believes it was all planned very deliberately and very cynically.

"People coming through that gate were people who didn't have to be in there but they were going to sit in that bus and were going to make sure that the little guys out there who were trying to protect their jobs by trying to stop a couple of janitors and secretaries from going in were going to get punished and make Suncor look like, 'Hey, this is why we had to lock them out, this is what we have to put up with.'"

Once the windshield had been smashed, the company, says Scott, could say that "this horrendous violence had happened. And the next thing you know we are in nationwide newspapers as the next terrorist organization of the century."

Suncor's request for an injunction was scheduled to be heard in Court of Queen's Bench on May 6, which may not have come as a surprise to Suncor, but it meant at least another week before access by vehicle to the plant could be guaranteed. Suncor managers had asked the RCMP to clear the pickets from the road but were told that the national "police force wishes to take a neutral position in the strike/lockout and do not want to get involved until the company obtains a court order." With the RCMP unwilling to act, Suncor began chartering helicopters to fly in parts and personnel. By May 3, at least six flights had been ordered and more were expected.

On the second day of the dispute, while there were more skirmishes at the plant gate and some of the picketers had taken to covering their faces with bags and balaclavas, another front opened up in the battle. Now both sides were attacking each other with great vigour in the newspapers. Suncor management told reporters tales of violence on the picket line while Marchand and his colleagues denounced the Alberta government for giving Suncor a $23 million tax break only a few days before the start of the lockout.

The Edmonton Journal ran an article that recounted the story of the bus rocking and of the smashed windshield. Marchand answered that the incidents were "provoked by the company." He said that the RCMP had told him they believed that the "rock could have come off of the tires." It's a wonder that the reporters

Marchand talked to took him seriously enough to print that nose-stretcher.

Ken Wagar, a member of MIOW's negotiating team, told reporters that the Alberta government was using tax dollars to lock taxpayers out of a job. He suggested his fellow MIOW members would have their revenge at the polls. A provincial election was scheduled for May 8.

Reporters immediately sought out the sitting Conservative MLA, Norm Weiss, who took the prize for the dumbest comment of the day.

"It will cost me some votes," Weiss admitted, "But only about 20 per cent of the people here are Albertans; their political interests are elsewhere."

Weiss was referring to the fact that the turnout in the previous election had only been about 54 per cent, but that ill-advised remark just about guaranteed that the turnout would be higher this time around. He seemed to be saying that living in Alberta, working in Alberta, sending kids to school in Alberta and paying taxes in Alberta didn't really make a person an Albertan.

While the picket lines at the main and north gates remained the focus of much media attention, MIOW's nerve centre was its union hall on the corner of MacAlpine Crescent and MacKenzie King Road. A fifteen metre by twenty-three metre, steel beam, two-storey building, the hall was where members picked up their strike pay, where the union executive met to plan strategy and where someone was always on duty to ensure the picket captains knew what shift they had drawn. Well before the start of the lockout, committees had been set up to coordinate publicity, picketing and dozens of other duties. Members were assigned to gather firewood for the picket lines, others were asked to arrange for a power plant to be hauled out to the site. A local company had already, on the quiet, given MIOW use of the trailers that were parked at the Suncor gates and local firms were being canvassed for other contributions.

The union had established, in short order, an effective infrastructure to address the needs of the membership throughout the lockout. Members needed to be called upon, to know they were essential to the union's battle plans. Because in those first few days, everyone felt their life had been turned upside down. They were all, collectively and individually, facing an uncertain future. There was no indication how long the dispute would last, much less whether they could reasonably expect to win even a modest victory. For the most part, they were all far from their hometowns and extended families. The cost of living in Fort McMurray was frighteningly expensive, moving out meant confronting enormous moving fees and, for those who were desperate to find temporary work, there wasn't much on offer. The lifeblood of Fort McMurray's economy is the production of light, synthetic crude and when 1100 people who were being paid good wages to produce that crude were suddenly locked out of their jobs, the entire community felt the collapse in purchasing power. From restaurants to hardware stores to real estate agents, there wasn't a business in the city that didn't suffer an immediate drop in sales.

While the entire city hunkered down in fear and expectation, the most wrenching dramas were being played out within the families of the union members.

Cal Morrison had hired on as a heavy equipment operator for Suncor in 1983. Two days before the lockout, he was in Edmonton. There a medical specialist sat him down to tell him that he had multiple sclerosis.

"The neurologist told me my attitude would make a big difference," Morrison recalls. "When it first started happening, my hand used to drop off the steering wheel. I'd be drooling, my cigarette used to fall out of my hand." But he was also told that because he was in his mid-40s, the chances of the disease completely crippling him were low. Still, it wasn't good news for a man with three children who was about to be locked out of his job.

Back home in McMurray, Morrison took stock. His wife Ramona was working and his oldest son had been, fortunately, laid off from Suncor, so he was drawing unemployment insurance.

"My daughter was twenty and in college in Lethbridge and my youngest boy was eighteen and at home. I had lots of insurance on me and I had a good talk with the doctor and he told me no need to go home and worry about it. So I had the attitude that my bills were all paid, I had a car loan, my daughter's tuition was paid for the year and I had enough insurance to help her finish her college. My wife was working. I had been through a strike in 1971 with the Teamsters and I survived that one. My wife wasn't working then and we had three small kids and we got through it. So I said I am ready for this one. I'm a strong enough believer in unions that I didn't get all upset about it."

That first week, though, Morrison didn't make it out to the picket line. He was at home, absorbing the news and gathering up the threads of his life. By the second week, "I was there," he remembers with evident pride.

Kirk McRae and his father both worked at the Suncor plant. Kirk had been at the plant for eighteen months when the dispute broke out. His wife Shannon had a job as a cook at the airport and they had a three-year-old and a six-month-old baby at home. They were living in a house they were buying from Athabasca Realty, the housing subsidiary of Suncor, but gave it up when the lockout began and moved in with Shannon's folks. Six months before May 1, Shannon's father, Al Davis, had told Kirk, "You'd better start putting your overtime money in a sock because a lock-out is coming." Al Davis was then a supervisor for Suncor and when Kirk and Shannon moved into his home, he was living at the Suncor camp helping to run the facility.

"At first, there wasn't too much tension in the house because my father-in-law was in the plant camp," Kirk recalls.

"But then he started coming home in the evenings and we started quarrelling."

One evening they had a shouting match in the driveway and Kirk jumped in his car and drove off.

"I was going to sleep in my car in the park. The police came along and asked me what I was doing. I told them about the fight I had with my father-in-law. So they went and phoned my home and discovered it was true. They came back told me they hoped I could work it out. After that we got on better."

Alvin Norman is from Pacquet, a fishing village in Newfoundland. In December 1982, he landed a job as a power engineer at Suncor.

Norman describes himself as the "kinda guy who don't like change. I like things the way they are." Yet he supported what he calls the "rah, rah leadership of Don. I thought he was doing a good job. When negotiations took place in 1984 I thought we were going to strike. I had my finances prepared. I thought we were going out. I made sure I had no bills, no new vehicle. I was renting. I was fully prepared to move into a smaller apartment if I had to. I was almost like a relief in 1986 to get it over with.

"I thought it was going to last a couple of months. I had two kids by this time. Shane was three and Shawn was two. My wife was behind me 100 per cent. I married my high school sweetheart. I saw the lockout as an attack on my family, to be honest with you. You can justify anything, I think, in defense of family.

"I stayed long hours on the picket line. My temper was up. I wasn't shaving. I wanted to take 'em on. Folks coming over for drinks in the evenings. We talked about what we were going to do. When the talk turned to violence, my wife kept reminding me of the kids. But looking back now, I was ready for violence. I wanted to be part of something, to do something. It didn't bother me. I don't know if you just lose your sense of reasoning or you just feel you have to do something to get back. I don't know."

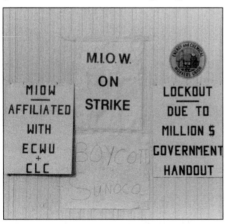

Union workers believed they were battling the company and the government too.

On many of those nights that he spent talking and drinking with his buddies, Norman often recalled an incident that had occurred in Labrador.

"If you get caught up in things sometimes you lose control. I remember being on a wildcat back in Labrador and I had a bunch of guys revved up so bad that I almost had them convinced to strip this guy off in forty below weather. He used to come out and taunt us on the line and we caught him. I wanted to strip him and send him back to town with no clothes. It was two miles to town. He'd have probably froze."

Brian Campbell, who in 1990 became president of the Suncor union, recalls that the dispute disrupted everybody's life. He wasn't prepared financially for a long lockout but he buckled down.

"I didn't lose my car. My wife was working part-time all along. She was sharing her job. She's a lab technician. She got extra work elsewhere too.

"I was a millwright by trade and Syncrude was looking for millwrights but I wouldn't apply. I said it back then and I'll say it now. I was committed to the cause and I was going to stay and fight the battle as long as I could and that's what I did. I was at the union office every day. I answered phones, I was on the constitution committee, I ran gasoline to the picket line. I was there to do whatever was needed. We weren't really organized starting off."

James Andrew (Jimmy) Cardinal is a welder from Lac La Biche, Alberta who accepted a job offer with Suncor in 1973. He apprenticed at Suncor and the company sent him to school to become a ticketed welder. Among the workers at the plant, he's a veteran who had, by 1986, been through plenty of labour trouble at the plant.

"The day it started," he recalls, "I went over to the picket line that morning. I wasn't so radical in 1986 because in 1978 we had a six-week strike. I was radical then. I was young, I was haywire. They locked the gates on us so we put our own lock on the gates so they couldn't open them, so busses couldn't come in. So they came to try to cut the lock. I was carrying a bat. I'd never hit anyone," Cardinal laughs and says with mock seriousness, "What, a guy can't play ball on the picket line?

"So they were trying to cut the gate open. They brought in a security guard named Hector and Hector got scared. And then my friend, John, whom I had worked with in mine maintenance and who had become a supervisor, came to cut it. I backed off. Anyway, a while later I get this letter from Suncor saying they had a photo of me carrying a bat and that they were going to sue me for

$2 million. Our president laughed at it and I tore up the letter. When I think back now, I wish I had kept it. At the time, I said, 'Where are they going to get $2 million off of me.' So in 1986 I kinda stood back and talked nice to everybody."

Cardinal, a guitar player and singer, says he did his picket duty but found it "so disheartening. There is nothing you can do. You see these vehicles go by, people giving you the finger."

Still, he was determined to stick it out as long as his finances held.

Over at the Colclough residence, Larry marched down to his bank the day the lockout began.

"You should have seen the line-up in that bank. A panic. There were other members there and businessmen. I walk in and there's got to be 250 people in there and I'm at the back of the line. Betty Agnew (the loans officer Colclough had seen well in advance of the lockout) comes out, she sees me, says, 'Larry, come with me.' So I walk around all these people and get the evil eye and she says, 'Ok, here's a program that I think you can afford. Are you ok with this?' And I says,'Yup.' Betty and the Bank of Montreal saved this house. All I had to do was pay the interest."

After he had squared away his mortgage, Colclough began his picket duty but found it stressful beyond endurance. He eventually shifted to duties at the hall. But the dispute intruded on every aspect of life.

Peggy Colclough recalls the day "Our oldest boy tried out and won a spot on the rep ball team. He came home with his uniform and put it on for his dad and dad said, 'I'd almost think this was a sick joke.' It was a Suncor-sponsored team and suit. But the coaches were really good. The coach was a Syncrude worker."

Bill Ross had years of union experience before he moved to Fort McMurray in 1974 and he was one of the veterans who was immediately drawn into the organizing activity before the lockout even began.

Married and with three children to support, Ross says he wasn't looking forward to the dispute and knew he and his wife, Leila, would have to plan carefully to keep abreast of the bills.

"We knew probably a month before. We started organizing committees, selecting picket captains, planning a food store, staffing the hall. I think the company was shocked that we had major money and a major union behind us. The company thought at the beginning that they could take us, that they could destroy the union. They had every intention of doing away with the union. But as the strike went on the support from our membership got stronger. Support stayed at 85 to 90 per cent almost right to the end. Which is awful high support.

"I was a picket captain and manned a desk at the hall. If there were any problems with the company at the gate we (the picket captains) were the ones who tried to settle it down to make sure no one got hurt. Our duty came up once a week or so."

Carl Cullihall, who started at Suncor in 1980, was in charge of strike pay and worked up the picket schedules. A former steelworker from Hamilton who had once experienced a nine-month strike and saw many of his colleagues lose their houses, Cullihall manned the phones, advising picket captains of their shifts each week.

"They had to do a shift a week, a six-hour shift. Strike pay was a maximum $200 a week. We used to pick up $25,000 cash every Thursday and we'd do the pay. We'd start at 8:00 a.m. and go to 11:30 at night. It was always the same people who did it. Out of of 1100 members maybe 300 to 400 did picket duty or anything we asked.

"My wife was working at the time. I was being hurt, but not as bad as some. I was with others who went around to the banks to explain to the management that we were locked out and that our members would pay when they could. What bank would be foolish enough to say, 'We are taking the house back?' They would have been sitting with 300 of them. They had to be reasonable."

Among the duties assigned, says Cullihall, was firewood detail.

"We had four guys the only thing they did was cut firewood. The whole time. Had to do something to stay warm. Also, at the picket line we had no electricity for the trailers so we had to buy generators, one for each gate."

Not a single vehicle, aside from the ambulances, moved across the picket lines for more than a week. By the third day, when the picketers erected a five-metre high plastic sheet across the road to shield their activities from the security cameras, Suncor bit the bullet and declared that all bussing to the plant would be suspended until the injunction was heard. The picketers declared a first victory.

The following day, Marchand told members that he and four others on the negotiating committee had been ordered to appear in court in Edmonton the following week for the injunction hearing. To buck up the spirits of those on the line, supporters trailed out to the plant gate for a barbecue. While they roasted weiners and hamburgers, 750 staff and scabs were inside running the plant and mine. The plant generally produced 50 000 barrels on a good day, but on the third day of the lockout it produced 55 000 barrels, Suncor's in-house newsletter announced. Outside, MIOW members were doubtful and rumours began circulating that Suncor was buying crude from Syncrude to refine or that Suncor was simply drawing down its reserves. The picketers accepted the wildest theories to explain Suncor's claim that production had never been higher. It was another slap in the face and heightened the tension not just on the line but across the city.

To ratchet up the tension just one more notch, Suncor lawyers filed a $5 million lawsuit against Marchand and the other members of the negotiating team. In the lawsuit's statement of claim, Suncor alleged that the company had suffered "severe and irreparable damage" because union members on the picket lines had engaged in intimidation, had issued threats and had unlawfully obstructed entry to the oil sands plant.

Asked to comment on the $5 million suit, Marchand made his wittiest comment yet.

"Is that dead or alive?" he asked. "I didn't realize I was worth that much."

The following day Marchand was in court in Edmonton for the hearing on the injunction. All the affidavits were presented and Suncor lawyer Brian Thompson argued that his evidence showed that "there has been a virtual blockade" outside the plant since the beginning of the lockout. Thompson, no stranger to hyperbole, said that the picket lines had sparked the "most serious incidents I've seen in my career."

According to *The Edmonton Journal*, Thompson said that the pickets had even built a fire in a drum and placed it in the middle of the road to prevent vehicles from passing.

MIOW lawyer Sheila Greckol answered Thompson's flight of rhetoric by telling Associate Chief Justice Tevie Miller that the fire was intended to keep the pickets warm and to allow them to cook food.

Thompson initially asked the court to prohibit any picketing. Later he changed his mind and asked for an injunction that would permit no more than five or six picketers at each gate. But Greckol said the maximum number of pickets should be set at fifty per gate.

"With only two or three people on a picket line in such an isolated location they will not be able to engage in the persuasion that is their lawful right," she said.

That afternoon, the injunction was granted and it limited MIOW to twenty pickets per gate. It also ordered them not to molest, threaten or intimidate anyone attempting to enter the plant, and to avoid any physical interference with vehicles approaching or leaving the plant gates.

Almost immediately after he left the court, Marchand found a phone and called the union hall in McMurray. He advised his colleagues that the injunction had been granted, warned that it was to be respected and insisted that no more than twenty members were to be on picket duty at any time. Word quickly went out to the line and careful counts were made repeatedly of the number of picketers on duty.

The injunction took effect on the date it was signed, May 6. Now the RCMP had a court order to enforce. The federal police began mobilizing immediately, and the following day more than 100 officers converged on the city to assist the local detachment. It would be a show of force, and the first display of that force would be on, of all days, election day.

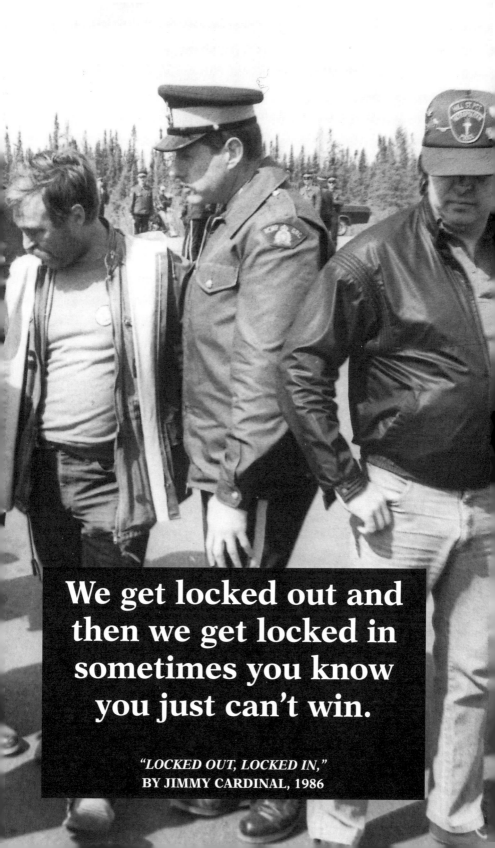

We get locked out and then we get locked in sometimes you know you just can't win.

"LOCKED OUT, LOCKED IN,"
BY JIMMY CARDINAL, 1986

"What in heaven's name would the RCMP be out on our picket line in battalion strength for?" (From l to r) Ian Thorn, Alvin Norman, Ken Partington, Jim Cardinal.

OVERLEAF: Eight days into the strike, MIOW workers are suddenly faced with a force of 160 RCMP, dogs and paddy wagons. An unidentified MIOW member is cuffed while Ed Vanmannen waits his turn.

CHAPTER FIVE

TEN BY TEN
ROW BY ROW
THIS IS HOW THE
ARREST SHEET GROWS

DAVE SCOTT crawled into his bed in the early hours of May 8. As a member of the union executive he had been putting in punishing hours sorting out problems and taking calls from picketers on the line, who had a two-way radio and called in frequently in a panic for one reason or another. Tonight he was looking forward to a decent slumber, but a couple of hours after he had stretched out, the phone rang. A jumble of rushed words tumbled out: he had to get out to the plant; the RCMP had 200 men on site with dogs and paddy waggons and riot gear and all hell was about to break loose. Scott, exhausted, was sarcastic, dismissive and unbelieving.

"What in heaven's name would the RCMP be out on our picket line in battalion strength for?" he asked his hysterical caller. Get a grip, he told the man and rang off. Minutes later the phone rang again. It was Marchand recounting the same tale. We're on our way over to get you, he told Scott, who was still half-awake and now fully annoyed.

"Twenty minutes later Don, Dan (Comrie) and Ian (Thorn) are pounding on my door. So out I went, and I remember we got up there and all you could see was a long line of RCMP Suburbans along the highway. And I thought, 'It's election day, and Suncor and the province of Alberta are going to make sure that those people inside the plant are going to be able to get out and vote.'"

Scott's bitterness was shared by every one of the several hundred MIOW members who showed up on the line that day. They started arriving throughout the night, and by daybreak there were several hundred members on site and many more en route. They were matched by more than 100 RCMP officers with dogs, riot

Several hundred MIOW members are matched by more than 100 RCMP officers with dogs, riot gear and bags full of plastic handcuffs.

gear and bags full of plastic handcuffs. By mid-morning they were arresting MIOW members ten at a time, cuffing them and placing them in the back of the paddy waggons for the trip to the RCMP holding cells back in Fort McMurray. For people there that day, it was a scene they all say they will never forget. They still talk about it as the event that shattered their illusions about fairness, democracy and the rights of working people. Watching the RCMP assist Suncor staff and scabs bus out to the polls to re-elect a Tory government meant one thing: that the government, the company and the police were standing shoulder-to-shoulder against working men and women. Even the most reasonable couldn't be persuaded to acknowledge that the election just happened to have been scheduled for May 8, a week after the onset of the dispute; that Suncor had gathered the evidence and gone into court and, in due course,

as quickly as was possible, had obtained an injunction; and that the RCMP had moved, with the dispatch demanded by the court, to enforce the injunction. And as far as the RCMP were concerned, the numbers assembled were necessary to ensure that no one got hurt. Which was exactly what happened. No one got hurt, and the injunction was enforced.

Suncor's Ron Wood says it really was coincidence that the show of force took place on election day.

"I mean we can plan, but we aren't that goddamn good. The agreement expired on May 1 and the election took place eight days later. We didn't orchestrate it to have an MLA elected," he says, guffawing at the suggestion that he plotted every move in concert with the RCMP and the government.

But to an MIOW picketer, walking the line at a plant surrounded by endless forest and muskeg, it all seemed so conspiratorial. They considered themselves peaceful men and women who had done nothing to justify such a massive show of intimidating force. And so they began stepping forward in successive waves to be arrested, to demonstrate that they believed the injunction was unjust, that they were not unreasonable people, that the only answer to an unjust law is to make a mockery of it. They allowed the busses filled with staff and scabs out to vote, but blocked them from returning to the plant. By day's end 121 MIOW members had been cuffed, driven to town, charged with contempt of court and released with a court date in hand.

Brian McFalls arranged for a babysitter for his kids that day, drove out to the plant and was overwhelmed by what he saw.

"I saw paddy waggons, trucks and so on lined up forever. It was a very strange sight. I wondered how they could manage to have all those police at their disposal so fast. We didn't represent a threat. We weren't the type of people who were going to riot in the street. There was no doubt who was on what side. I had no doubt before but now it was sure demonstrated. I remember a bumper sticker I once saw that said: 'I used to be disgusted. Now I'm just amused.' That's sort of how I felt."

Larry Colclough recalls stepping forward that morning to be arrested and having the plastic cuffs put on.

"They put them on so loose that we had them off by the time we got into the paddy waggon. Colin White borrowed an RCMP officer's hat, and we got a picture of him wearing it in the waggon. We were polite and well-behaved."

Colclough shared his paddy waggon with Jimmy Cardinal.

"Ten of us would stand in a row and they'd pick us up and another ten would take over," Cardinal recalls.

"I got picked up and Marvin, this RCMP friend of mine, said 'I'll take that guy.' I said, 'Marvin, you know I'm not going to hit you.' And Marvin said, 'Yeah, I know.' So later I'm sitting there in jail, in one of the drunk tanks and there's about ten of us in there. And I started thinking, 'Can you imagine. First we get locked out and then we get locked in.' So I wrote a song and everybody just loved it. We knew we couldn't win. That's the way General Robert E. Lee felt. Can't win the war but keep fighting anyway. The company was at least forced to recognize that we stood together and that we were fighters."

Raymond Lays recalls being arrested by "this big dude and he just tightened those ties right down. All the other guys slipped out of theirs but I couldn't get out of mine. The guys ribbed me all the way to town. But I didn't say anything to that officer. Man, he was a big dude."

After his release, Raymond says he "drove right back out there. I felt like telling those cops, 'Sure, take me again if you are that stupid.' They (the RCMP officers) had been brought in from all over. There was one young guy there from the Northwest Territories who told us, 'Man, I don't even want to be here.'"

Watching her husband being hustled into the RCMP wagon, Pamela Lays says "Raymond was the last one in. I followed them into town. That night the kids saw, on the TV news, the guys being arrested. They didn't see their dad. But what do you tell a five- or a six-year-old when daddy's got to go out and do his picket duty?"

Before Ray's arrest, Pamela and her sister-in-law and all of the kids had driven out to the line.

"We weren't going to go all the way out, but once you get near there is no place to turn around. We had all the kids with us (including her own four children). We saw cops lined up along both sides

Home away from home. The union's base camp offers a tarp for protection against inclement weather, and is shielded from security cameras by a five-metre high plastic barrier.

of the highway. I had to drive past to find a place to turn around. I couldn't believe it, couldn't believe how many of them there were."

Even Suncor's Gene Bacon was disturbed by what he saw from the inside of the bus on voting day.

"On May 1 I had very little information about what was happening on the line. I was living in camp and working long hours. It wasn't until we went out to vote that I saw it. I knew a lot of those people. It was disconcerting. I found it disturbing to see that many police officers, to see so many people I knew cuffed and being carted away. I'd heard through the mill that there was a contingent of RCMP up there at the gate, but I had no idea there were that many. The RCMP weren't housed at the plant. They brought busses through the line and held exercises here. But I never saw an RCMP officer down in the camp.

"It bothered me personally that people were exposed to that – to see people in the community cuffed and carted away. Some saw it as humorous. But these were members of the community."

Alvin Norman remembers his arrest was a matter of awkward formality.

"Most of the cops were pretty good. They cuffed me. I said to the cop, 'Buddy, where the hell do you think I am going?' He said, 'Yeah, you're right.' And he made them really loose so I took them off when I got in the van. He was an older cop. I found the older ones were more mature. They didn't have anything to prove."

Norman says the moment he got home "I picked up the phone and I called my father (in Newfoundland). He said, 'What have you done now?' I said, 'I got arrested.' He said, 'That doesn't surprise me. If you'd done anything different I'd have been disappointed.' Whatever that meant. I think what he meant to say was that he was happy I was standing up for what I believed in. I didn't want him to hear about it from someone else.

"My wife knew I was going to get arrested. I just had to get someone to the picket line to get my car. It was funny too. There

After being booked, workers pose for a photo inside the jail. (From l to r, back row) unknown, Steve Walsh, Larry Colclough, Mark Hogan, Jim Cardinal, Peter Seddon. (From l to r, front row) Kevin Peters, Keith Jordan, Wally Chiasson, Levi Garrett.

was almost a fight to get arrested. They were taking ten at a time. The cops saying, 'No, no, you've got to wait until we've arrested this bunch."

Throughout, the RCMP were clear with the press about the behaviour of the picketers.

"There has been only passive resistance," Staff Sergeant Wayne Carroll told reporters, "There has been absolutely no violence at the picket line."

Marchand was much less restrained when he spoke to journalists.

"This is the action of a police state," he told the local newspapers, "I've never seen anything like it in all my life."

Marchand said the mass arrests were a gross violation of his members' civil liberties. And he accused the government of pressuring the police to get tough with MIOW members.

"So they bring up this army and they haul all our peaceful members off to jail."

Despite Marchand's provocative comments, RCMP spokesman Staff Sergeant George Lettett insisted that the force was "striving to maintain a neutral role. We respect both positions...We're ensuring that the number of people on the picket lines does not exceed the limit and that there is clear passage of vehicles through those lines."

Throughout the day Suncor officials kept clear of the press and the confrontations. Their story was that the arrests and the presence of the RCMP had nothing to do with the company. In Suncor's internal newsletter, company officials told staff and scabs in the plant that Suncor was not paying the RCMP for its services and that it was the federal police force itself that determined the number of officers stationed at the gates. It was a prudent public position to take but it certainly wasn't one that was shared by the company's own security staff. One security guard said later that it was a tremendous relief to have the RCMP show up. The guard said the picketers were so numerous that Suncor's security staff often felt threatened.

Neither the picketers nor Suncor knew how long the RCMP contingent was planning to stay on-site. As it turned out, the contingent remained for less than a week. When they left, the rumour followed that they were the main body of a special riot squad assembled for duty at Expo '86 in Vancouver, which opened May 2. When the quiet returned, the local detachment resumed its duties, which meant an officer or two on the line most days and some nights.

During the days that the special squad was stationed at the Suncor gates, 152 MIOW members were arrested, Tory MLA Norm Weiss was re-elected by the slimmest margin ever and the RCMP overtime bill amounted to about $207,000. In addition, it has been estimated that the cost of each arrest – the cost in court time, legal bills, paperwork, etc. – came to $600 to $800 per arrestee. That's another $100,000. Add to that the cost of transporting the officers to McMurray and housing and feeding them, and the final tally for responding to the perceived threat at the Suncor picket lines could well total close to $400,000.

That seems an awful lot of money to have devoted to ensuring free passage in and out of the plant gate. That thought must have occurred to the judge whom the picketers appeared before a month later. He found them guilty but "waived any penalty or sanction." It seemed that the most enduring impact of the police action was the unification and radicalization of union members. The massive show of force helped eliminate the middle ground in the dispute. Those who had been neutral before were now either solidly behind their own union or, in the case of a small group of dissidents, firmly behind the company. Riding the wave of anger that was generated by the arrests, MIOW leaders wisely chose to channel that sentiment into a public display of strength.

You cannot hope to bribe
or twist, thank God the
(Fort McMurray) journalist

But, seeing what the man
will do unbribed, there's
no occasion to.

HUMBERT WOLFE

Many families were facing bankruptcies; the march was a tonic for everyone.

OVERLEAF: Spirits are lifted when the wives organize a march down Franklin Avenue, the whole length of Fort McMurray. MIOW members are reminded of their size, their cohesiveness and the backing of their community.

CHAPTER SIX

POISON PENS

ON A SATURDAY morning, ten days into the dispute, 2000 MIOW members and their families and supporters gathered in a light rain in downtown Fort McMurray. As they assembled, many expressed astonishment at their numbers. Scattered in neighbourhoods throughout the city, it wasn't often that they had the opportunity to gather in a large group to reaffirm a common sense of purpose. They set off from the Plaza Two parking lot on Franklin Avenue and began a slow march to the MacDonald Island Recreational Complex. Their mood mounted as they marched.

SUNCORRAL – ROUND THEM UP AND LOCK THEM OUT read one of the forest of signs carried by the men, women and children. IF SUNCOR DOESN'T CARE, WHO DOES? read another, this one tied to the chest of a grade-school boy. SUNCOR, WHERE PEOPLE ARE OUR MOST DISPOSABLE RESOURCE. The signs were grim reminders of the economic distress most of the families were suffering. But marching together was, many agreed, the tonic that was needed.

The idea for the march came from the wives, Marchand told a reporter as he joked with the crowd surrounding him.

"All our wives got together and decided to show Suncor we are all united. They said, 'Suncor has brought in their army of 160 policemen, they put handcuffs on our husbands and Suncor should see we are together.' I'm so proud to be president of this union."

Diane Jordan, the wife of a Suncor mechanic who was marching with her son, said "Suncor figured, after six days, we'd all go back to work. But we are sticking together. All we are asking is to keep the contract the way it is, but they aren't even willing to do that."

Jordan also said she was upset about the letters Suncor was sending workers who were renting or buying company houses. The letters said everyone would have to continue making rent or mortgage payments.

"They've taken our jobs and now they're going to kick us out of our houses if we don't pay rent."

More than 2000 people march to show their support for the locked out MIOW workers and to protest the use of non-union workers at the Suncor plant.

Alvin Norman, a power engineer, said he and his fellow members were prepared to stay out as long as it took.

"We're not taking the shaft Suncor is giving us...We don't have a million-dollar P.R. (public relations) department. We've just got the workers."

Theresa Keeping, whose husband had been locked out of his job as a machine operator, said she was protesting Suncor's use of non-union workers.

"They're bussing just anybody in there to take their jobs...We should go back to the bargaining today. Why not? Instead they're bringing people in from out-of-town to do the work."

The march boosted flagging spirits, allowed people to express their outrage at the police action and demonstrated to the entire community that the workers and their families were reasonable, peaceable people. While they marched, busses were crossing the line at the plant and would continue to do so for the remainder of the dispute. It chafed at and rubbed raw the pride of the locked-out workers and would provoke many of them to rash acts. The injunction had opened the line, but at considerable expense to the police, to the reputation of the company and to the influence of the moderate voices within the union.

Before and after the march all union members received in the mail from Suncor a Record of Employment Form. This mailing set off rumours, once again, that the company was preparing to fire everyone. And once again Suncor had to dampen the flames of rumour, telling many disbelieving union members that the Unemployment Insurance Commission required them to provide the form to all locked out workers. The flare-up revealed the extent to which the company had expended its credibility. People were prepared to believe the worst.

The stalemate in the dispute had a rippling effect on the community. Now workers who could foresee no end to the battle began searching for work elsewhere or thinking of moving. Workers with children were prepared to wait until school was out, but others began pulling up stakes. The rising tide of panic caused housing prices to drop like a stone. *The Edmonton Journal* reported that 157 houses purchased from Suncor's real estate subsidiary,

Athabasca Realty, had been given back to the company by workers who couldn't continue to make payments. One man said he lost $7,500 on his house and Rosalyn Houlihan, whose husband was a millwright at the plant, said their $140,000 house sold for $122,000 just before the start of the dispute.

Raymond and Pamela Lays and their four children had by the time of the march moved into her parents' house. They weren't paying rent and were trying to get by on strike pay of $200 a week. But one of the children had medical problems and every trip to see a specialist in Edmonton cost them money they didn't have. The less they had, the more frantic they became.

Brian McFalls and his wife left their house and moved into a cheaper apartment.

"It was the pits," he recalls. "Our dog kept going back to the house. We ended up storing stuff for friends who moved out of town. We had two barbecues, two sets of patio furniture, an air conditioner and a water bed. We had quite a little setup there until we ran out of money. When we moved to the apartment we shifted the stuff to other people's places. We had tickets to Expo '86 as well, but we decided we couldn't go, and we sold them."

Perhaps the most enterprising of the locked-out members was the group of Maritimers who drove to Edmonton and bought used school busses. Back in McMurray they took out the seats, packed in their household goods and headed back to their hometowns.

If people were packing up and leaving, a good part of it was due to the struggle of trying to survive in Fort McMurray on strike pay. The city is a northern town, and the cost of living there is well above the cost of living in Edmonton or small towns close to Edmonton. The financial crunch came quickly for even those who had prepared for the dispute. There had been talk of setting up a food store to help reduce the cost of household expenses for the membership. Now, clearly aware of the growing desperation of many members, the union executive formed a committee to get the store up and running as quickly as possible. While a group of organizers contacted food wholesalers, others prepared the bottom floor of the union hall for the storage and sale of everything from corn flakes to coffee. The idea was that the store would be open on the same day that members received their strike pay, ensuring that the money they got upstairs could be spent downstairs before any of it went missing in, say, a tavern.

Carl Cullihall, the man in charge of handing out strike pay, said a limit was set on food store purchases.

"You could spend your $200 and that was it. One time we found one guy buying $200 of one thing. It turned out he was buying it for his restaurant. He could buy that item cheaper from us than he could get it from a wholesaler. We put a stop to that."

Suncor power engineer Bill Johnston and his wife Edna ran the food store.

"Don (Marchand) got the idea for the store," says Bill.

"We bought wholesale and sold at 50 per cent of that. Not everything sold at 50 per cent, not the lower priced stuff. After the lockout, the Safeway and IGA people said that if it had lasted any longer, it would have pushed them under. Before the lockout started Don went to Safeway and IGA to ask them to give a break to members. They said no. Later Safeway donated stuff and even lent us grocery carts.

"The store was open three days a week, right after strike pay was distributed. Our union hall had a full basement, part of which was our food storage area and store and another part served as a food bank for the city. People would make their purchases and we'd put them out back where they could drive around and pick them up. Sometimes people from the food bank would just drive up and pick up our food instead.

"That store brought people together. It was vital. We had to deal with people complaining. Some wanted us to sell smokes and diapers. But we sold only the essentials. There was great variety. Fresh fruit, vegetables, no flour, but tea and coffee and eight types of soup."

Even now, eight years later, the posted prices at the food store seem an incredible bargain. Corn Flakes were 75 cents a box, Kraft Mayonnaise 88 cents a jar, Sunlight dish soap 86 cents, toothpaste $1.01, tomato soup 31 cents a can. Everyone asked about the food store talks about how it brought people together and put food on the table at a time when it seemed impossible to feed a family on strike pay.

Larry Colclough found picket line duty too stressful and so he was reassigned to duty at the food store.

"That was enlightening. I got to appreciate the troubles people were having. You knew who was hurting and who was well-heeled."

Colclough says some union members "never set foot in the place. Some found work, some moved to other places and said give me a holler when it's done. So there were some members who never collected a dime in strike pay. There were also some who were working and complained that they couldn't shop at the store although they weren't giving their 10 per cent. (Any member who found a job was asked to donate 10 per cent of his or her income to the strike fund.) My function was to help members who needed it. Then there were people who were so proud they wouldn't go up to the food store. I remember one guy did his picket duty and almost starved, but wouldn't shop there."

Occasionally, someone would come in and it would be clear that they were in dire need and Colclough would quietly add food to their order and then, unspoken, slip it into their car out back. In the end, the operation of the food store cost the union about $200,000, but its value to the members was incalculable.

Brian Campbell said initially he didn't agree with the idea of setting up a food store. But he soon changed his mind.

"That store saved all of us, me included. When I went in there I didn't spend what the union allowed me to spend. I had four mouths to feed. I never spent more than $40 and always had enough food for two weeks. It might have gotten a little out of hand near the end with the steaks and other meats. But by then people needed a treat."

Pamela Lays, who had four children to feed, says she shopped at the food store whenever it was open.

"We never ate so good."

The one bitter memory Pamela retains about the food store had to do with her attempt to get the union to bend its rules to help out a needy family.

"If you worked you were supposed to pay 10 per cent of your wages and you could buy groceries. Well I paid Ray's 10 per cent but there was a family we knew up here, lived in a trailer. Had two little boys and one little boy was sick and was going to Edmonton for an operation. They were going to lose their trailer. They were behind on their land taxes. I went up one day to the food store and I took my friend with me and they told her she couldn't get her groceries. She was doing her husband's picket duty because he had just gotten a job on the crew that was widening the road out of town. They wanted 10 per cent from her but she didn't have it. She didn't have any money and they wouldn't let her buy groceries. I told them I didn't think it was fair. There were people donating their picket line money back for those who needed it. And these people didn't have any money. I mean everybody's union up to a point, but Jesus you still have to have a place to live. And come hell or high water that man would not let her go in there. They eventually lost their trailer. When lockout was over they had bills coming out of their ears."

Raymond Lays shakes his head at the memory of the family.

"We were lucky compared to them. They had it bad."

But aside from the occasional dispute about rules, the food store was a beacon of light in a stormy sea. No matter how financially strapped, people always knew they would have food for the family.

The opening of the store didn't address all anxieties, though. There were rumblings of dissent and, on May 13, in surely what was the most misguided, knuckleheaded intervention thus far in the dispute, the editors of the local newspaper, *Fort McMurray Today*, published a letter that was signed "Concerned and Worried Employees from Both Staff and MIOW." It is a cardinal rule of the newspaper business that letter writers must sign their names to their missives. Allowing anonymous letters into print is to invite libelous comment, irresponsible spleen venting, manipulation of public opinion by stealth and unfair attacks on public figures. In this case, the newspaper allowed anonymous interests to attack the union without fear of having their motives examined along with their comments. When a doctor writes to a newspaper to defend the principle of extra billing, readers can decide for themselves what merit to assign to the argument given the physician's obvious financial interest in billing his patients. Imagine the same letter signed by, say, a grateful heart surgery patient who believes his surgeon deserves to be rewarded for his skill. Whether you agree with the argument or not, the patient's motives for writing give an authority to his letter that the doctor's letter lacks. *Today's* editors were later to defend themselves by stating that they themselves knew who the letter writers were and that, since they were satisfied that the letter, and others that were to come, were authentic, they decided to allow the authors to state their sometimes intemperate views without having to take public responsibility for them. It was a dangerously wrong-headed decision that had an enormous impact on public debate within Fort McMurray for the duration of the dispute. It introduced a rogue element into what had been a sharply divisive but open and democratic discourse about the dispute. Now, someone was commenting on the dispute and, in some cases, taking cheap shots at the union leadership, under a cloak of secrecy.

That first letter stated that the authors were a group of "50 and getting close to 100 and still growing" who wanted "our men and women back to work and our lives back to normal."

The letter praised "the good men already out there trying to pick up any work at all and the even better ones (who) will be leaving town – they choose not to sit around on a picket line (or should we say drink coffee, play cards, have weiner roasts)...Not all the females support the 'circus' (the march) that was on Franklin Avenue!"

The letter expressed a legitimate point of view but it did it in an anti-democratic fashion. For many, it was a hurtful attack on the integrity of those who believed they were fighting for a democratic right and for the very survival of the collective bargaining unit. A day later, a second letter was sent to the newspaper and to the union office, this one signed "MIOW and ashamed of it." This one called for another vote on Suncor's last contract offer. The author was clearly in a rage.

"There are contractors out there doing MY work, and a lot of us have gone to the point of getting the ball rolling and are seriously considering getting busses to take us into work! I, for one, am tired of caring (sic) the load for guys who have bad job evaluations, have the flu 30 times a year – I'm a tradesman and I have worked for ten years with Suncor – it's been a good life and this community is our home – and we're NOT prepared to get our pink slips in the mail, and have our jobs taken over by the MANY unemployed out there."

Those were fighting words, and they provoked the incendiary Pamela Lays, a woman who describes herself as "mouthy," to answer. In her letter she literally kicked to pieces the pious arguments of the "Concerned and Worried Employees":

> I would like to know where you got your information that the picketing and display was exciting. I sure don't think it was nor does my husband and the other union members who go to picket.
>
> We all know our bills won't stop, at least ours haven't. As far as it being fun, I haven't found a funny thing about this situation since it started.
>
> Who are you to say my husband is not a good man because he spends six hours out of ten days on the picket line (standing up for job security)?...
>
> Why do you call the march held on Saturday a 'circus'? I didn't realize we all looked like a bunch of animals. I marched along with the other 2000 people with my head held high, proud that my husband is man enough to stand up for himself and expect a proper living.

Her letter to *Today* was signed "Not afraid to sign my name, Mrs. Raymond Lays," and after the dispute ended she cursed herself for not giving her name as Pamela Lays.

Pamela's letter caused a bit of a sensation within the community. It was so surely aimed that many union members congratulated her for saying what she did, when she did. She found herself besieged by telephone calls and well-wishers who greeted her on the street. There were a few who chided her for her comments and a couple of retrograde men who thought her place was in the home, quietly taking care of her four children and steering clear of public comment. But for the most part her letter gave many a much-needed psychological boost.

After the publication of the letter, MIOW members held a barbecue a downtown park to rally sagging spirits. All the local supermarkets generously donated food, and three pigs were roasted, one of which was named Mike Supple, Suncor's vice president of the oil sands group. While members and their supporters were feasting, Jimmy Cardinal and his group, The Strayngers, played his song, "Locked Out, Locked In." Each verse was greeted with wild applause, and Cardinal sang himself hoarse.

Little emotional boosts were becoming more and more essential. Although the dispute was only two weeks old, its impact was already being felt within the local business community. The Macleods store announced that week that it was closing, the local cable company said it had lost 300 subscribers and a moving company said that in the first two weeks of the lockout, it had moved thirty-five to forty families out of town.

Those statistics put enormous pressure on Marchand and his colleagues to show some flexibility. But how to get Suncor back to the table?

Initially, Marchand had insisted that Basken and the ECWU stay out of the negotiations and the dispute in general. But now Marchand thought Basken might be able to help.

"I didn't dare get involved without Don asking," Basken recalls.

"But finally Marchand called and asked if I could do something. I didn't know anybody in the company. I phoned some people I knew in the oil industry in Edmonton and asked who I should contact at Suncor. Then I phoned Suncor and said I wanted to meet with Mike Supple, Suncor's vice president of the oil sands group. I told the Suncor people that Supple should phone some company people I had worked with and some company lawyers who I had worked with so that he could satisfy himself that it wasn't a phony meeting and that I was trustworthy."

Eventually, a meeting was set up in Toronto.

"I met with Supple at a hotel to explain to him what the arrangements were between ECWU and MIOW, and how we would be supporting the lockout," says Basken.

"I told him I felt that we had to negotiate the agreement because in McMurray, there were so many vicious feelings both ways. I said I would put someone in there to assist the local, a senior person from my staff, and asked him (Supple) to meet with ECW and see if we could work out the actual arrangements before they went back to the bargaining table in McMurray.

"There was no legal role for us. We weren't legally representing MIOW. The local had just voted to affiliate with us, and that's a rather informal arrangement between the local and the union. I had to convince Supple that this was a legitimate arrangement under our constitution, and I said that he would be wise to meet with us. He was very sceptical. He said he would think about it. I tried to convince him that it was in the company's and the membership's best interests that we do so. To the best of my knowledge he contacted other people who knew me, and then we got together again."

A second meeting was set up in Edmonton. At that meeting Supple brought Ron Wood, who by now was working with a pared down negotiating committee of three: himself, Gene Bacon and a third member of the human resources department, Vaughn Hibbits. Basken brought along R.T (Buck) Philp, a union veteran who was to play a key role in resolving the dispute. Basken said Philp, who died some years after the dispute ended, would relocate to McMurray for the duration to lead the bargaining.

Suncor management had been given Philp's name before the meeting. Gene Bacon said discreet inquiries had been made.

"Obviously, we checked him out. We'd heard his name. He had a solid reputation. We heard he was a no-nonsense guy and that showed quickly. Buck was definitely a professional."

Marchand was wary of Philp but delighted to hand over contract negotiations to someone else.

"He took over negotiations, which I didn't care for. He was a good man."

Buck Philp was then national programs coordinator and secretary treasurer of the ECWU. Born in Medicine Hat, Philp's first job was with the railroad. During World War Two he was in the navy, and when the war ended he went back to the railroad. By

1950, though, he was working in the oil industry, and five years later he was in the thick of union politics. Sending Philp to McMurray was an inspired move. Philp had by then dealt with every major oil company, had negotiated more agreements with more players than even the most experienced Suncor executives.

MIOW's Comrie recalls no one in the union knew who Philp was when he arrived. They had been told that he was a trouble-shooter and that he was well respected.

"Buck became the chief spokesperson and it was very difficult for Don," Comrie says.

"Don and Buck went head to head. Of the whole committee probably Gary (Morrison) and I were the first to recognize the capabilities of Buck. He was a likeable guy in his late fifties. He was comfortable in the union hall. He had only been there a week when guys started coming up to him and talking to him in the hall. Members got comfortable with him right away. He could drink and play cards, and get up in the morning and go back to the bargaining table."

"Mom, please don't vote PC again," reads one of the many signs carried down Franklin Avenue in Fort McMurray. (From l to r) Gladys Muise and Ruth Anne Hilderly.

One of the first things Philp did was to reorganize the bargaining committee. He whittled it down to himself, Thorn, Marchand, Comrie, Dave Scott, Ken Waggar and Gary Morrison.

Thorn says the new committee "was much smaller than the previous one. The guys on the new one plus a whole bunch of others were on the old committee. Dan and Gary led the strategizing. They, more than any of the others, understood what it was about. Don understood the situation but he was still trying to rebel against it. Buck led the negotiating and Don very willingly sat back. Don may have given the pretence of leading but it was really Buck, Dan and Gary."

Scott says although he remained on the committee he and Philp didn't get along.

"He thought I was too political. I had a hard time with him because he wouldn't tell me what was happening. But he was a good guy. He knew what he was doing and he was a good negotiator."

Once the new committee was in place, Philp put out feelers to Suncor and on May 26, almost a month into the dispute, both sides met to resume negotiations.

While Philp took over the talks, Thorn was detailed to work on the grievances.

"There were 367 that I had put in my hands," Thorn recalls.

"I spent hours and hours on them, sometimes with Buck. We couldn't arbitrate them all. Some of them weren't even issues anymore. In going through them I would make proposals. On some I would consult with Buck and he would take them home for the evening and come back and make suggestions. We ended up arbitrating five or six and I presented the arbitrations on those. Most were discharges, terminations of employment. The employer alleged cause. I don't think we won any of the five. They were pretty serious offenses. One was related to alcohol, another to sleeping on the job. By the time the dispute ended, there were only a half dozen of the grievances left unresolved."

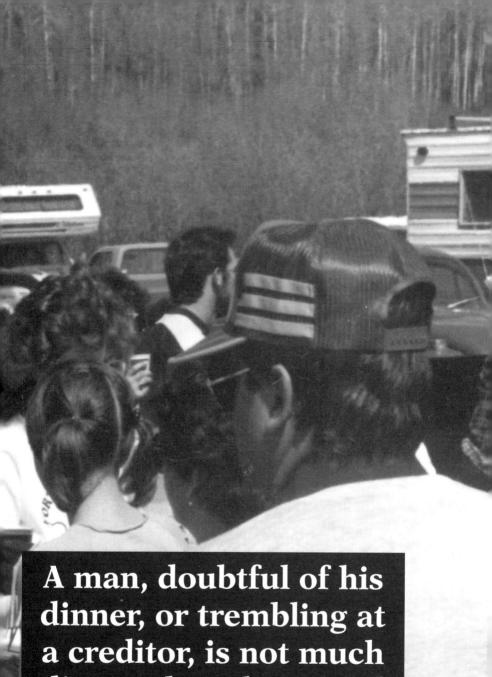

A man, doubtful of his dinner, or trembling at a creditor, is not much disposed to abstracted meditation.

SAMUEL JOHNSON

The barbecue helped boost the morale of the MIOW workers. Above, one of the Edmonton organizers of the pig roast.

OVERLEAF: In a show of support, the Edmonton-based Dandelion Political Action Committee holds a pig roast to boost morale. (In hat, serving drinks) Emmett Travis. (In baseball cap, back to camera) Roland Lefort.

CHAPTER SEVEN

OUTGUNNED AND OUTFLANKED

WHILE THE COMMUNITY tore itself apart, and workers and their families pinched pennies and agonized about whether to stay or leave, inside the Suncor plant it was all harmony and efficient, productive labour. The in-house newsletter was filled with reports of hockey scores and birthday congratulations and the number of injury-free days and, most impressively, the daily and weekly tally of the barrels of oil produced. By the time both sides sat down to resume negotiations at the end of May, the company was reporting daily production at 60 000 barrels and up. The plant, according to the company, was routinely breaking its own past production records.

For the union, those numbers were like a boil that needed to be lanced. There were two pilots within MIOW, and between them they made daily flights over the complex to assess what was happening inside. Their reported observations fuelled talk that the company was fiddling the production numbers. Others say that from the perimeter they could see what was happening in the mine and could see the smoke from the refinery, and none of them were prepared to believe that Suncor was making more oil than it had been able to make when MIOW members were on the job.

Ron Wood insisted that the record output was attributable to thorough preparation.

"We had people in from Sarnia, that was our prime resource. We also had people from Sun Oil out of the US. We had a lot of resources and we improved production. I know the story going around was that we were doing so well production-wise because we had put in a pipeline with Syncrude and were using it to get stuff from Syncrude to be processed. That was ludicrous. Syncrude would never get involved in a situation like that. Yet that (rumour) sold to many union members. It is easy to prove that we were telling the truth. But the union didn't want to admit that. You can imagine the position that the union leadership would be in at that time knowing that their members were out on strike and that the plant was more productive without them. I think it was a combination of really good preparation and the technical expertise to do the job. It was incredible."

While the strikers and their families waited for news of the strike, Suncor brought in scabs to replace them.

The frustration of the picketers mounted along with the production numbers. There were incidents on the line or in town almost daily. At the same time, Marchand ran a verbal war on tradespeople who were crossing the line.

The tradespeople crossing the line told the MIOW pickets that they had contracts with Suncor, and refusing to cross the line would be illegal and cause for dismissal.

"This is the reality of life in Alberta," Vair Clendenning of the Alberta and Northwest Territories Trades Council told Marchand and his colleagues. There were expressions of support and donations from Syncrude workers, from the Alberta Union of Provincial Employees and from many others. But for every expression of good will there seemed to be a counterbalancing expression of anti-union sentiment. Late in May, a quarrel between pro- and anti-MIOW tradespeople almost escalated to blows in the Boilermakers Union hall in Edmonton. Thirty-four boilermakers had signed up to work at Suncor. Boilermakers Union leaders said they were legally obliged to put out a call for boilermakers, but that none of the members had to accept the Suncor job offers. The scuffle between those eager to go and those who were ready to punch them out was widely reported. In McMurray it ignited the touchy tempers of the weary and financially strapped MIOW pickets. What made the situation so volatile was the evidence that many other tradespeople were crossing the line as well. Local Teamsters who drove for Diversified held a one-day job action to support MIOW, but they too said they were contractually bound to drive or risk losing their jobs.

Marchand made the rounds of union halls talking to fellow leaders, but it didn't seem to make much difference. Suncor had more than enough willing and able workers eager to bunk in camp and take home big paycheques.

Brian Campbell spoke for many of his colleagues when he said that the "biggest problem I had with the scabs is that in the building trades in Edmonton, in their hall, they were fighting for the work, to come up here. They knew they were going to go inside and make a bundle. They are the ones I despise the most. They just couldn't wait to cross our picket lines."

Just as Marchand was attempting to shame other unionists into respecting the MIOW line, the picketers received word from the Unemployment Insurance Commission that they were not eligible for benefits. It wasn't an unexpected judgement, but it irritated just the same. Each day seemed to bring more news of another institution or agency or interest that was lined up against them. The feeling of isolation provoked defiance, and the picketers began taking more risks.

Throughout June there were incidents on the line and in town. Truck windows were broken and the cable leading to Suncor's security trailer from the light plant was cut. On June 10, there was a "rock concert" at the main gate. Stones were thrown at twenty-six busses that entered that morning and roofing nails were scattered in the road to flatten tires. In town, the RCMP arrested and charged a MIOW member for kicking a car. Another member was arrested and charged with throwing a rock at a car. Some mornings MIOW members would wait by the road out of Fort McMurray and throw rocks at the busses as they passed. Many of the members were finding themselves capable of actions that were, they thought, completely out of character. Or maybe they were discovering that, given the right circumstances, anyone, even the calmest and most rational person, can lose himself to the moment.

Alvin Norman had by then moved out of his apartment.

"We stored the furniture at a friend's house. We were living out of suitcases with relatives in Edmonton. I was coming back to picket. It was hard on the kids. That's what really got me bitter. Then I was really pissed off. I was really angry. For the first time in your life you were caught up in the circumstances. You couldn't do anything. You try but you go out and watch the busses going through. What's the point of having a strike if you can't stop scabs. One morning at the picket line the cops wouldn't even let me park on the road. It just blew me away. My father spent five years in the war fighting against that kind of tyranny and as far as I was concerned they were putting it right back in."

Norman said he "didn't have any animosity toward company supervisors or secretaries. I just thought it was part of their jobs.

It was the guys the company brought in, the scabs. We had a guy who lived across the back alley. Before the walk-out started he'd be working on his cars and I'd take him over a beer. Two days before the lockout he took a staff job. He was a scab. In my opinion he was the worst kind of a scab. He took the job to avoid the inevitable. I remember him getting on the bus one morning after the lockout started and me and big Gerry Snow were standing on the corner watching – I guess it was intimidation on our part. We didn't say anything, but he went to work and said he had to run for his life for the bus. We were just standing there."

Before the lockout, the Suncor busses would pick up workers in town at assigned stops in every neighbourhood. Now the people being picked up were Suncor staff and scabs. Norman said MIOW had "people going out to the bus stops. There was harassment. No doubt about it. The police clicked right into it and they were there before we were. They'd stand there and watch us so we couldn't harass very well. We also picketed the Sunoco gas stations. I always enjoyed that. It would be such a moral victory when you'd see people who had pulled up for gas decide not to buy any. Or if you heard of a guy working inside the camp who just decided to quit because he couldn't be part of it any longer. I don't even know if it was true but I sure believed it. I needed to believe it."

Dan Comrie says by now many of the busses crossing the line were "beat to shit. There wouldn't be a window or a tire left. Guys had made broom-handles with a spike on the end. All of this was done in Suncor shops before the lockout started. We weren't new to strikes. Busses were attacked on the highway with ball bearings fired from slingshots. Managers' houses attacked. Some managers moved their families out of town.

"Buck used to get angry with us. He'd say 'Don't fucken do that.'"

But within some of the picket teams, the feeling was that if the stakes were being raised, then the tactics used would become rougher.

Before the line was opened with the injunction, Comrie said he found out that scabs were being choppered in from the city airport.

"We went out to the airport. The pad's way out on the tarmac. A couple of times we charged the tarmac. It scares the shit out of them. In all fairness to those tradesmen, they didn't know. Some of them got out, shook our hands and left. Other guys would get flown in, see the chopper and say, 'What the fuck?' Suncor wouldn't fly them back to Edmonton if they quit."

Brian McFalls says the drill on the line was to "get as close to the vehicles as possible to let them know we sure weren't in favour of them crossing the lines. That was the most we could do."

The provocation that triggered many incidents was "scabs putting their paycheques up against the window," said McFalls.

"That really was annoying. That was the sort of thing you never forget. The majority of them fought to get on the side of the bus where they wouldn't have to face any of the picketers but there was the odd one that really enjoyed his wretched role in the dispute. Some of them were in management."

One day, McFalls says, "a guy was driving up quite quickly. Somebody smashed his windshield and the look on that guy's face as he tried to reverse out of there. It was a look went from smugly superior to terrified. I believe it was a chair that was used to smash the windshield. That guy's transmission was probably never the same."

Another time, a car came through, said McFalls, and "somebody on the picket line recognized the car and told an RCMP officer that he should check it out. The mountie checked and lo and behold the guy was in trouble. When he came back out the gate the police told him he couldn't drive his car. It was to be impounded or something. We told him he could leave his car with us, that we'd look after it. For some reason he didn't believe us. He had to beg for quite a while before they'd let him drive into town."

The scene at the isolated north gate was less frantic but even there the picketers were capable of engaging in games that had the potential to go wrong.

Kirk McRae says many nights at the north gate "we'd shoot grouse with slingshots. We used the slingshots on security vehicles as well. Then somebody brought out a .410 shotgun and shot a grouse, but there was so much buckshot in it that it was uneatable. We used to roast the grouse up there."

At the time it never occurred to the picketers that having a shotgun on the line might be taken the wrong way by either the RCMP or Suncor's security staff. Wiser heads eventually prevailed and the shotgun went home without the SWAT team making an appearance.

Another time McRae says a "security vehicle drove in and we crept around behind it to try and drop a tree into the road to block its exit. But that didn't work. The vehicle went out too fast."

From the end of May to early July the negotiating committees met twenty-six times. Although Wood and his fellow negotiators were willing to talk with Philp, they gave no indication that they were willing to budge. Oil prices were still plummeting, light crude was flowing from the plant in impressive volume and the company kept pushing as hard as it could. Basken, keeping himself abreast of the progress of the dispute, was privately convinced that Suncor management "believed they could get rid of both MIOW and ECWU."

Wood, who by then had grown to respect and like Buck Philp, denies there was ever any serious consideration given to breaking the union.

"Union busting is a thing of the past. In labour relations, it doesn't happen any more. I mean really. My dad was with the United Mineworkers out at Nordegg. He was on the union side and was very aggressive. So I heard the union perspective all my life. So when I went into management, I knew both sides."

But Bacon, who worked closely with Wood on the negotiating team, is much more equivocal when asked whether there was intent to break the union.

"Those rumours persisted (that Suncor wanted to rid itself of MIOW) and I can't categorically say there was a foundation for that. But in any labour dispute in that era, and even in Alberta today, it would not be unusual for a company to take the approach that if they were going to have a dispute, then it's going to be a good one. It's a fairly common approach in labour disputes here (to break the union). I guess it is similar to the position Suncor takes today with various interest groups: if it becomes too expensive to do business with that group, then there are alternatives."

Philp's approach to negotiations ran contrary to Marchand's approach, which was a clause-by-clause examination of each element of the contract. By contrast, Philp sought an overall agreement. That made perfect sense to Wood.

ECWU's "shell agreement is something like three pages long," says Wood. "You see, everything you put into an agreement is a restriction on management."

So the simpler the agreement, the happier Wood and his colleagues were likely to be. But Marchand thought it all a mistake.

"Buck just talked the full collective agreement," says Marchand.

"That gives the company a big advantage. A contract is quite complicated. If you take it section by section, you don't get screwed up in language. Buck's approach is exactly what the company wanted."

But Comrie, who had been on the MIOW negotiating team long before the dispute started, said the problem that plagued the relationship between the company and the union was that MIOW wasn't consistent.

"In all fairness to the company," said Comrie, "we'd agree on the language but it wouldn't be written up very well and we wouldn't be off the bargaining table for two weeks, even though we knew the intent, and we'd have a grievance in right away and have to get an arbitrator to settle. And Buck just finally said, 'The language we do here, that'll be the language. We understand the intent and that will be the intent.' And Ron Wood said, 'It's never been in the past.' And Buck said, 'I don't care what it was in the past.' He says, 'Put me on the stand. I'll tell the arbitrator. If the local's wrong, they're wrong. That's the way ECWU operates. Our deal is our deal. We don't go back on our word and we don't expect you to.' So those kinds of statements really started to affect the committee. We said, 'If we agree to something, why don't we agree?'"

As the talks went on, the MIOW negotiating team began rallying to Philp's view, accepting his conviction that they had to give, had to recognize the company's right to manage, while not folding on basic matters of principle. But still Wood and his colleagues stood firm, not bending an inch. If the hiring of the scabs was nudging the picketers to violence, the violence was in turn hardening the position of the company. By now Peter Pocklington had locked out his unionized employees at the Gainers meat packing plant in Edmonton and there had been plenty of violence on the line there. It seemed that nightly, television news carried images of riot police chasing and subduing the Gainers workers and their supporters.

Given the atmosphere, it wasn't surprising that negotiations broke off July 2. According to the union, the unresolved issues were overtime pay, vacation pay and wage increases.

"We proposed an economic relief package in recognition of the low oil prices which the company rejected out of hand," Marchand told the press.

"The company told us they were having trouble managing the overtime. So we said we'd leave the overtime as it was and allow the company time to straighten out their management systems. The company didn't even want to talk about it. The company says it only wants temporary economic relief, but they want the contract changed permanently."

Ryan Moore, Suncor's manager of government and public affairs, said the company and the union had gotten to a point where they were haggling over contract language that affected the day-to-day operations at the oil sands plant. Moore said shift scheduling turnarounds and grievance procedures were examples of issues that the two sides were unable to come to agreement on.

"Basically, Suncor wants new language in the contract to cut down on the excessive and repetitive number of grievances filed by the union," said Moore.

The day after Marchand and Moore sparred in the press, Marchand pulled another cat out of the bag. He told a *Fort McMurray Today* reporter that Suncor had presented the union with a return-to-work agreement that stated anyone convicted of a picket line offence would be dismissed. That agreement, said Marchand, applied to the 152 people arrested on election day.

"The company is saying they don't have a job."

"Furthermore," said Marchand, "the company is insisting that the same penalty be applied to people who engage in harassment of staff employed by or for Suncor.

"Anybody who shakes a fist, waves a sign, or flashes a finger while on the picket line could lose their job over this," said Marchand. "We talked about a return-to-work agreement at the table. We presented our side and they threw this document at us and said that was it, they didn't want to negotiate at all."

Suncor answered Marchand's inflammatory remarks with a press release.

"This document (which Marchand had referred to) appears to be a preliminary document tabled at negotiations," the press release read. "This document has not been dialogued at the table. We are therefore not prepared to comment on it as we do not want to prejudice negotiations on its final outcome."

The day after that exchange, labour union members and leaders from across Alberta made their way to the Suncor plant to show solidarity with MIOW. The unionists were organized by Gary Shury, an official with ECWU based in Edmonton. Shury, who was also vice president of the Alberta Federation of Labour, brought up Gainers workers as well as leaders from a half dozen other unions. The group vowed to put pressure on the Building Trades Council to sanction the MIOW picket line.

"There will be further meetings with them and we are not giving up trying to get their support," Shury told MIOW members and reporters at a press conference.

On July 7, both sides met again and Suncor submitted to the union a formal proposal. The bargaining committee responded by scheduling two meetings to present the offer to the membership. Almost immediately after the meetings Marchand told the press that the offer had been rejected, in a show of hands vote, by 99 per cent of those who had attended the membership meeting. Suncor spokesmen said they were disappointed, but refused to make any further public comment about the vote.

But Marchand was more forthcoming. He said the return-to-work agreement put forth by Suncor was still offensive in that it specified dismissal for anyone convicted of picket line offenses or anyone involved in harassment.

"I'm upset at the company's last offer," said Marchand, "for the simple reason that they must think we are a bunch of yo-yos."

With talks once more suspended, Marchand, Philp, Comrie, Thorn and several others flew to Saint John, New Brunswick, for a week-long ECWU conference. Marchand said he planned to lobby delegates to support a boycott of Sunoco gas stations. And just before departing, Marchand said he was prepared to cancel his trip if Suncor showed the slightest interest in returning to the table.

"We don't have to go if the company is willing to sit down and negotiate," Marchand told *Today*.

Almost as soon as Marchand left, Suncor issued a statement that MIOW negotiators had walked away from the table and had presented to their members a company package that had not been finalized. Furthermore, company spokesman Wayne Antler said, the abrupt departure for New Brunswick of Philp, Marchand and the others meant that there would be no return to the table until they had made their way back from the Maritimes. Antler's comments left Marchand in a rage. The day he returned to McMurray, Marchand said he had called Suncor before leaving town and was told that the company negotiating team was on vacation.

"That's a lie," Antler retorted hotly. "Our negotiating team took the weekend off, and that is allowed."

It was a juvenile exchange, and it reflected the personal animosities that seemed to be the greatest obstacles to a settlement. Aside from picking fights with the company, Marchand said he had accomplished a great deal in New Brunswick. "A boycott of Sunoco was now underway," he said.

"There are 35 000 members (of ECWU) out there with their families and friends, and if that doesn't put pressure on Suncor, I don't know what will."

But Suncor had a new angle of its own. The company spread the word to the local newspapers and the local MLA that MIOW had not allowed its members to vote on the company's last offer. This prompted another nasty exchange in the newspapers and convinced many unionists that the newspapers were in the company's pocket. The nasty feelings simmered until July 25 when MIOW was told that the company wished to clarify its offer of July 8. Both sides met that day and the company delivered a copy of what it called its "final, final offer," an offer that was not subject to negotiation or change.

When Philp saw the proposal, said Comrie, "he told them, 'Don't put the offer because we will turn it down.' That really took the company on. Then we went back to the office and Buck said, 'Let's roll up our sleeves and get this out to the whole membership.' We sent out a statement to everybody."

But even before they had made it back to the union hall, a local radio station was announcing that the company had made a new offer. That broadcast and the "final, final offer," which was no more acceptable than any of the others, angered the negotiating team. They agreed to organize a membership meeting and to recommend that the offer be rejected. While calls were being made to the members, Philp sat down and drafted a statement which concluded: "Your Negotiating Committee unanimously recommends TOTAL REJECTION of the Company's proposals."

As members streamed into the meeting the following day, copies of Philp's document were handed out to everyone. The document noted that the company was proposing to reduce vacation pay, to cut the pay of those transferred, to expand the management rights clause, to give non-bargaining unit employees the unlimited right to perform bargaining unit work and to start charging employees for bussing. As for the back-to-work agreement, the document stated that the proposed agreement was "unacceptable."

As the meeting began, a member said he had heard Suncor had a letter it was sending out in the mail to all employees. He moved that the meeting be delayed until all members had received the letter. The motion was voted down and Philp took over and went through the company's proposal. His remarks were followed by a government-supervised vote on the offer. Eighty-one per cent of the members voted to reject.

Suncor's response to the vote was terse. Suncor's offer "reflects the economic realities of operating the oil sands plant...as far as Suncor is concerned, negotiations are complete," said spokesman Ryan Moore.

According to Neil Reimer, the membership's rejection was a key element in solving the lockout. He says that with the clear support of the membership, Philp now had the strength to request that Basken begin talks with Suncor at a higher level. "It was a common strategy," says Reimer. "When talks were stalled at one level, we would attempt to solve them at another level. But this strategy could only be successful when the union had the clear support of the membership."

With the talks in limbo, both sides withdrew to retrench and plot strategy. After a short period of reflection, a period which saw more "rock concerts" and other incidents on the line, the union decided to stage a public event. They organized a benefit dance for members and invited Dave Werlin, president of the AFL, and Nancy Riche, a vice president of the CLC, to attend and address the gathering. More than 350 people, including a group from the Gainers plant, turned out for the dance. During the evening, Werlin told them that what was needed, more than anything else, was a change in Alberta labour laws.

"Employers can hire scabs, give them permanent jobs and force people to take action to protect the jobs they left when they went out," said Werlin.

"That kind of situation causes desperation and it leads to people taking a stand. And as soon as you take a stand, they call the cops. They go to that slot machine they call a court, they pull the handle and out pops an injunction."

For her part, Riche said the CLC would work to widen the Sunoco boycott.

"There is an unofficial boycott of Sunoco stations in the East now, but we are going to make the Ontario government (which then owned 25 per cent of Suncor) aware of our intentions of an official boycott," Riche told cheering members.

The evening created a small media splash – in part because ten tires were slashed on cars outside the dance hall – but it didn't do much to relieve the worries of the membership. And as strategy went, it wasn't exactly a telling blow.

Meanwhile, the company was plotting something much more elaborate. It was a many-pronged assault and, at first, it didn't appear to be anything more than a series of unrelated events.

On August 1, Suncor announced that the plant had recorded its second best month of production in history. And Wayne Antler said the company was hoping to set an all-time record for production in August. His remarks were clever and disarming, but nerve-rattling.

The production records, he said, were the result of new equipment and an all-out effort by the plant's workers.

"It all started about March, and I think it is due to the millions and millions of dollars we invested in the plant here over the last couple of years."

No, it wasn't just that the replacement workers were better, ran the subtext of his remarks, it was the investments as well as the fact that the replacement workers were highly motivated.

Marchand attempted to laugh off the numbers, but they had been tossed into the marketplace of ideas and they created doubt about the wisdom of the union leadership in continuing to oppose concessions.

At about the same time, the company returned to court to renew the injunction and this time, the judge ordered the picketers to remove all objects from the access road and to stand in the ditch to picket, and it forbade them from using any noise-making device or carrying anything in their hands except picket signs or articles for personal comfort.

Then a small ad appeared in the classifieds of the local paper: "Suncor employees. Should you stay out any longer on principal only? Principal put on the table doesn't give your kids a bit of nourishment nor satisfaction. Please send your thoughts with your name, employee number to Box 234, c/o *Fort McMurray Today*...We will report the results back to you – Suncor Concerned Responsible Wage Earners."

At the time, it seemed the work of dissidents. But as the unsigned letters began appearing again in the papers, and other elements of the company's strategy unfolded, many questioned whether the ad was really paid for by dissidents. And if it really was paid for by dissidents, then was the company delaying talks in an attempt to promote further division within the ranks?

While those questions were being asked, Suncor unexpectedly filed an unfair labour practices complaint against MIOW. Company spokesman Wayne Antler said the negotiating team had misrepresented the company's last contract offer and had not been bargaining in good faith. Philp, Marchand and the others were flabbergasted and enraged by the move. Now there was no question of going back to the table until the complaint was heard, at the end of August, by the Alberta Labour Relations Board.

Dave Scott, the most volatile member of the MIOW negotiating team, said the day the complaint was filed was the "first time I got physically mad. I felt like the company was laughing at us and that the province was supporting them. I thought it was a total cheap trick. They wanted rid of the negotiating committee. They were trying to tell people that we weren't telling the truth. It was like somebody had told Fort McMurray, the place where I live, where I have to walk down the street, that I was a liar. That's what that meant. I didn't like that. That was unjust. It was character assassination."

On the heels of the complaint, Suncor sent letters to all members outlining the last contract offer, spelling out in detail the impact the proposal would have on their jobs. And finally, almost as soon as the members had the letter in hand, management officials began meeting privately with civic leaders, businessmen and local politicians.

Added up, it was an impressive offensive. And it left Philp fuming. Suncor, he charged in a newspaper interview, was trying to turn MIOW members against its negotiating team.

"They want to paint a bad picture of the union executive to undermine the bargaining committee...The company's charges (in the labour practices complaint) are frivolous. I think they are stalling in the hope that they can go around the committee and get another vote on their last position."

And sure enough, two days later, *Today* ran another anonymous letter, this one signed "Concerned MIOW Employees."

The negotiating committee hasn't done much for workers, the letter stated.

"Do you not think it is time to wake up and smell the coffee?"

Bad times have scientific value. They are occasions a good learner would not miss.

RALPH WALDO EMERSON

Buck Philp was a union veteran who played a key role in resolving the dispute. "Members got comfortable with him right away," a MIOW member said later. "He could drink and play cards, and get up in the morning and go back to the bargaining table."

OVERLEAF: Serious consequences for serious actions: MIOW workers leave the courthouse after their arrests for breaking the injunction. (From l to r) unknown, Eric Lummerding, Paul Zwicker, Jim Tittman, Ralph Finch, unknown.

CHAPTER EIGHT

THE SHOCK TROOPS

BUCK PHILP MAY HAVE been angered by the unfair labour practices complaint but he wasn't nearly as upset as Basken was.

"I was absolutely livid that they should charge Buck with bargaining in bad faith. The company was still convinced that they could get rid of both MIOW and ECWU. There were a lot of things happening, and I think they carried it right through to the final settlement," said Basken

All the letters and the appeal to dissidents "were orchestrated," Basken believes. "The company was orchestrating little groups of people here and there to get them prepared to go back to work without MIOW or ECWU. That's why the proposal was made on the 25th of July to be taken back to the membership. The idea was that we would get caught recommending rejection so they could say, 'See, the union doesn't want to settle.'"

At the same time, someone also floated a rumour that ECWU was holding out for a better deal so they could sell it to Syncrude workers and draw them into the ECWU as well.

That, says Basken, "was a figment of somebody's imagination. Buck and I never even discussed that. Who could have been responsible for such a campaign? Let's put it this way, it wasn't done without Ron (Wood) and (Mike) Supple knowing about it. See, they weren't convinced after the 25th that they could negotiate a deal with us. If they were, why the hell did they charge unfair labour practice and defame Buck? That was the biggest disgrace of the whole thing. To defame a guy who had negotiated thousands of collective agreements and had a reputation beyond reproach. I was prepared to call CEOs from corporations that Buck and I had dealt with over the years to go before the labour board to vouch for Buck. That would have been difficult, but I am positive that a number of them would have come. Buck had always kept his word.

"I took it personally because they weren't taking us seriously, and they were trying to get rid of the union through a labour board case which was clearly not true. And they were picking on the one guy who had the credibility among the membership up there."

The company's offensive likely did provoke more splintering within MIOW, and more and more dissidents, still under the cover of anonymity, began speaking out. The company had time on its side despite the fact that it was costing Suncor as much, if not more, to run the plant without MIOW. Those who were working were banking heaps of money. Wayne Antler himself acknowledged that the company's payroll bill had not decreased. What was happening, a local investment adviser explained to a reporter for *Fort McMurray Express,* was that more money was being funnelled into fewer hands. The advisor, Melissa Vanrey, said the people who were working were either investing in big ticket items – things like vehicles, jewellery and exotic vacations – or investing in mutuals and tax shelters. "Business is definitely up for us," she said.

At the same time, with the dispute now into August, members were thinking about school in the fall and where the money would come from for the little necessities. City council had just voted against giving strikers any relief on their property taxes, and it was clear that the talks wouldn't even resume until the end of

August at the earliest. The dog days of summer had arrived with a vengeance.

The steady accumulation of frustrations provoked union members to a new pitch of fury. Throughout August, while their television screens were filled almost nightly with scenes of violence at Gainers, MIOW members lashed out. Throughout August, tires were punctured, bus windows smashed and gas stations in town were picketed. Once, members even thoughtlessly set up a picket outside the RCMP station.

"This guy calls me at the union hall," Dave Scott remembers, "and says an RCMP sergeant says you've got to get your ass down here and stop the guys from picketing the station. They are interfering with the police and all that. I burst out laughing. Here we are in the middle of a dispute, and our guys are picketing the police station. I thought that was funny. We got those guys out of there not now, but right now."

Cal Morrison says by August there was a dangerous restlessness on the line. Part of it was boredom, part was anger. And all of it meant trouble.

"Me and this other chap Gilbert Faucher, we used to drive up and down the road, go up to the north gate," says Morrison.

"We'd stop at the lookout point where they had a security guard and we'd drive him crazy. We'd drive and throw rocks at signs. One night there was some contractor's equipment parked. They were doing some work on the entrance to the lookout point. Gilbert and I started messing around, not doing any damage. We knew the guy who owned the equipment. We just got on, I started up the Cat and security came down and threatened to call the mounties and throw us in jail. We told him to go to hell. And that was that. After it got dark, at another spot halfway between the lookout point and main gate that the security guards used to sit at, we used to stop and turn out the lights. They couldn't see us. We'd throw rocks at the blades of the Cats and the guards would come down the hill again. They weren't very good security. Gilbert would get out of the station wagon about 200 feet back and make noise. One night there was four security guys around this equipment and I hollered, 'Gilbert get on the other side of the road, tell

117

the guys to come up the other side.' And Jesus, the guards went crazy. They all jumped in the pickup and took off up the hill."

Another night, Morrison got a couple of new mounties in a jam.

"There were two mounties just out of boot camp and we got talking to them. They had an old Suburban parked there. It was 2:00 a.m. and we told them, 'There's nothing happening. Go get forty winks. Jesus, the two of them fell asleep, and at 5:00 a.m. Staff Sergeant Wally Nicklin showed up and said, 'Where's the boys?' Did he tear a strip off those poor bastards. We told them later we didn't mean to get them in any trouble. Jesus, they didn't trust us after that. But we used to get up to pranks. We'd put nails in the road for the trucks. We used to stand shingle nails up with our feet and trucks would go over them. It wouldn't affect the tires until they got a couple of miles away.

"And the busses, when they went by we would squirt ether in the air conditioning. It screws up the air conditioning pump. You just squirt it in the grill. The mounties caught onto us pretty fast for doing stuff like that. But the nails, we used to get away with the nails."

Raymond Lays says for the picketers, the worst moments were when scabs came out after putting in a shift. One day, Lays remembers, "me and a buddy saw a cab taking a scab through the gate. My picket duty was finished so we jumped in the car and followed him downtown. We followed him to town. Got into the back streets. The guy wouldn't get out. We'd pull up and sit on his bumper. The guy must have told the cabby to go on. They'd go a little farther and we'd pull up again right on his ass. We did that for about three-quarters of an hour. The guy must have racked up some bill. The scab wouldn't get out. He was scared. We finally left because my car was getting low on gas."

By August, more wives were doing picket duty for their husbands, some of whom had found part-time jobs. It was a new experience for most of the women, and prompted many to get more involved in other aspects of the union's work.

The fiery Pamela Lays began joining her husband Raymond's picket duty. Raymond said the women injected a new fighting spirit into the teams on the line.

"You get the women out there and it was different. I remember she was with us one cold night. We were all sitting inside and Pam comes in and says, 'Get out here now, the goddammed busses are coming in.' And she got everybody out again. But you know after three months on the picket line you're kind of drawn out. And the women, I found, they weren't losing their temper, but they made everybody get up and start moving. I remember another time Pam grabbed a cop's megaphone and started screaming, screamed right in his ear."

Pamela is quick to add that "it was an accident. I was waiting for the busses. I didn't realize when I grabbed the megaphone that it was on, and I screamed and he was standing in front of me and I just about deafened him. I never saw a cop jump so fast. He threw his hat and he cursed and he swore."

Pamela said Raymond eventually got a job with a construction crew in Fort McMurray – a job Raymond describes as one of the worst he has ever held – and she took over all his picket duties.

The more she was out, the more nervy she got. One night a scab held his pay stub to the window of the bus, to taunt the picketers, as he came across the line.

"I threw a rock and smashed a window, but I never got caught because I was so short the cops couldn't see me. It made me angry. Here, I didn't have enough money to take my daughter for an ice cream."

Bill Ross, one of the picket captains, says "the women were harder to control than the men. We had four or five women who came out. I had to tell some of them to pull back."

Aside from picket duty, the women provided much needed moral support. Dave Scott said being on the negotiating team was a thankless task and "when wives came up and said, 'You are doing a good job,' that would keep you going. The wives formed an association and they became the strongest supporters. I couldn't believe some of those women. When it seemed there was no end to it, they'd be around to keep people going."

Don Marchand said he was at times overwhelmed by the positive role many wives played in the dispute.

"My job was to let the members know what was in the

proposed agreement. I'll never forget, one time two ladies came to me in the office and asked why I recommended turning the company's (July) proposal down and I went through the agreement and the women listened and wrote notes. And then they wrote a letter to the newspaper."

The letters from union supporters were a vital addition to the public debate. With more and more unsigned letters appearing every week, all of them aimed at those who were financially stretched to the limit and uncertain about the course their union was pursuing, the message from supporters gave the impression that there was intellectual vitality within the union ranks. On August 19, two letters appeared in *Today*, one from each camp.

"We feel positive that the ECWU has more in mind then (sic) just the Suncor employees," read a letter signed, 'Concerned Responsible Wage-Earners.'

"If its intentions are to organize Syncrude, it certainly can't do that without negotiating an attractive (Syncrude-persuading) package for MIOW," the letter concluded.

The letter questioned motive, made cheap allegations and attempted to drive a wedge into union ranks. All under the safe cover of hidden identity. If it was company inspired, then it had maximum impact and created the damage it intended. If it was the independent work of union dissidents, then it was misguided and inept. The dissident view had as much legitimacy as any other. But to organize that view into a coherent force, someone had to assume leadership responsibility. In the absence of an identifiable leader, the dissidents did nothing more, with those letters, than aggravate a bad situation and further weaken the bargaining power of their own union. By contrast, on the same day, Brenda Ashley had a letter published in the same newspaper. Its effectiveness stemmed not just from its careful wording but from the fact that it was written by someone with the courage to lend her distinctive voice to a public debate.

"I can appreciate Suncor's disappointment at the rejection of its last offer," Ashley wrote, "but a vote was taken and once again Suncor is out of line in trying to force a second vote. As a matter of fact, I was disappointed in the result of the last federal election. Perhaps you would cry a little for me too, and get me another vote until I get what I want."

Rumour is a pipe
blown by surmises,
jealousies, conjectures.

WILLIAM SHAKESPEARE

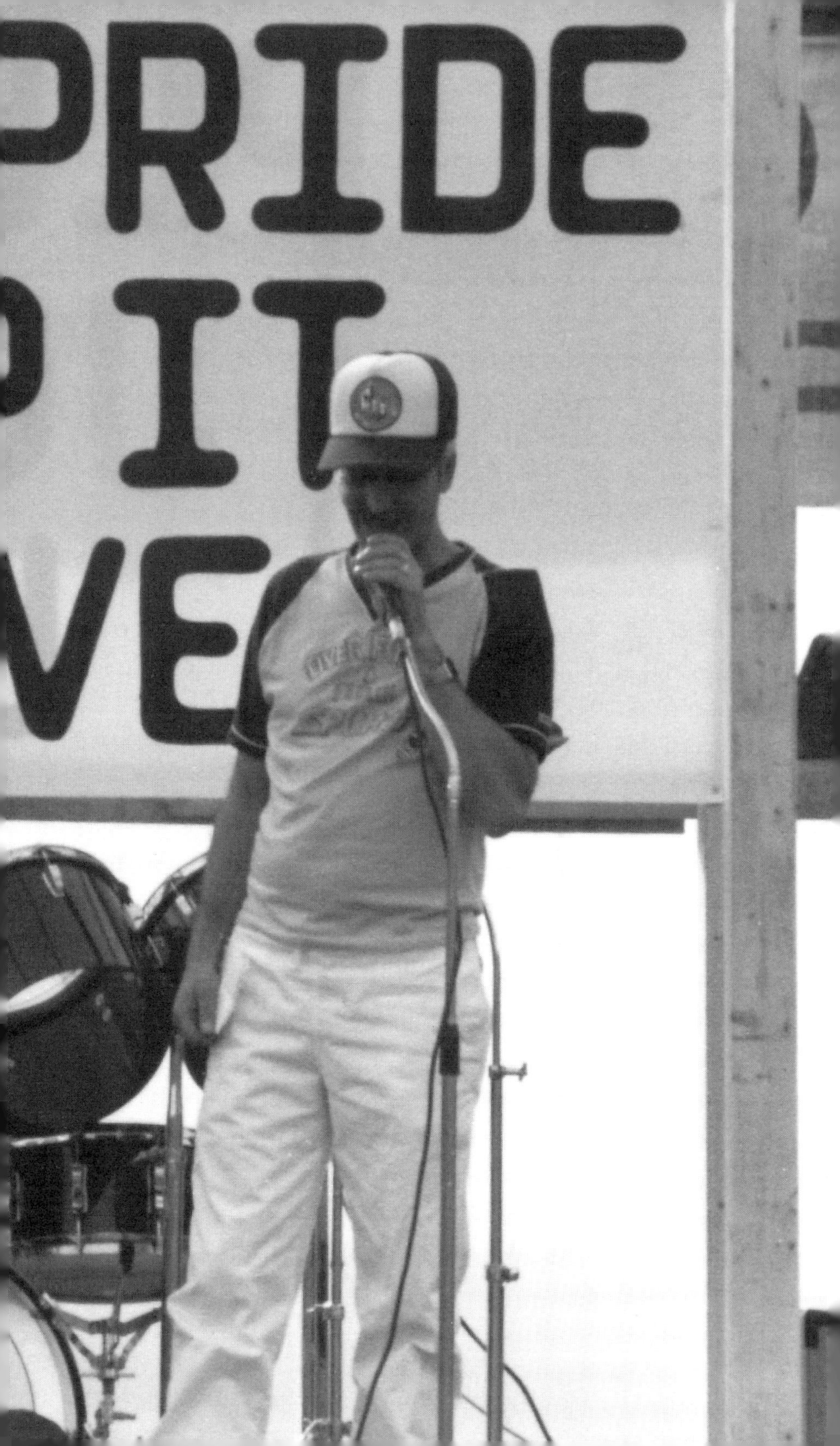
PRIDE

Support from outside the community showed MIOW workers that their struggle was not being waged unnoticed. Photo shows members of Edmonton's Dandelion Political Action Committee.

OVERLEAF: With the dispute dragging on and letters sniping at the union appearing in the local newspapers, union pride was difficult to maintain without frequent shows of solidarity. (From l to r) Ann Dort MacLean, Provincial New Democrat candidate and Don Marchand, president of the union.

CHAPTER NINE

DAYS AND NIGHTS AT THE RUMOUR MILL

TWO DAYS BEFORE the Labour Relations Board was set to begin its inquiry into Suncor's complaint, the MIOW negotiating team made another offer to the company. Company officials looked at it and, before even calling MIOW to say it was not acceptable, revealed to the media that it had been rejected.

"Unfortunately, the union's response was inconsistent with the company's final offer in a number of fundamental ways and was rejected," company spokesman Ryan Moore told reporters.

The statement took MIOW by surprise.

"We haven't talked to them since we discussed our package last night," an astonished MIOW spokesman Gary Morrison said when called by reporters. "We were hoping they would consider that package."

The package, said Morrison, contained changes in monetary issues.

The offer was an appeal to stave off the inquiry into Suncor's complaint. MIOW leaders knew the inquiry would consume a great deal of time and money. They were confident that they would be exonerated, but still the inquiry would stall the dispute at a time when MIOW members needed, desperately, to see some sign of progress.

At the end of August, it took two days of hearings in Edmonton for three members of the Labour Relations Board to conduct the inquiry. Both Suncor and MIOW were represented by counsel. Suncor's complaints were that MIOW had failed to make every reasonable effort to enter into a collective agreement and that the union had misrepresented to its membership many elements of the company's offer. To prove its case, Suncor called to the stand all three members of its negotiating team as well as two MIOW members who had been at the July 26 meeting when Buck Philp and Don Marchand had recommended rejection of the contract offer.

MIOW member Robert Cameron, a three-year employee and MIOW member, said he had volunteered to testify. He said that the MIOW publication he was given as he entered the meeting was lacking in detail. He said that when he later received in the mail a copy of the company's explanation of the offer he became "really upset."

The second MIOW member, Lewis Broda, said the explanation of Suncor's offer that he received in the mail "hardly seemed like the same document" that he was handed when he arrived at the meeting. Both men were critical of the manner in which the offer was presented, and Suncor lawyer Brian Thompson made much of the fact that union members themselves were speaking out against both the leadership and MIOW's bargaining committee.

But MIOW lawyer Sheila Greckol said the complaint was not about union dissidents, and that for the hearings to focus on dissension within the union was to engage in pointless "muckraking."

All in all it amounted to a nasty, expensive squabble between parties that neither trusted nor believed each other. Several years earlier Greckol, who had handled by then hundreds of grievances for MIOW, had told Marchand that he needed the expertise of a larger union. In his book on the ECWU, Wayne Roberts quotes Greckol's frustration with the situation at the plant.

"It was really a war," Greckol told Roberts.

"It was like nobody was home at the shop. The overtime was incredible. That led to drug abuse and ravaged families. There was a lot of theft, vandalism, time-wasting. Employees just weren't working like they would for an employer they respected. The local didn't give an inch, nor did the company. Bringing a lawyer into those situations is at best a Band-Aid. You need to resolve those situations on the shop floor. Lawyers just bastardize the process."

So Marchand had finally brought in the expertise of a larger union, and now Philp and the ECWU were grappling with the poisonous feelings that had accumulated between the two parties.

When the hearing ended both sides made their way back to Fort McMurray, deeply uncertain about how the board would rule. The board had promised a decision within two weeks, and while they waited, Suncor invited MIOW to a meeting to clarify the union's position on several issues. The meeting was brief, and when it ended both sides went back to their corners. The waiting was nerve-wracking. And while they waited, two local politicians entered the fray.

Tory MP Jack Shields publicly called for independent observers to pressure both sides to settle. He attempted to strike a statesmanlike pose, blaming both sides for the impasse. But his dislike of the union got the better of him and he lashed out at ECWU, suggesting that the national union's involvement in the dispute was an obstacle to a settlement. Then he got to the nub of what was really bugging him. Shields said the dispute was destroying the community. As an example of the damage it was doing to the local economy, he cited his son's restaurant, O'Reilly's, which had just shut down after losing $20,000 a month. Shields said he was a shareholder in his son's restaurant and pub. So Shields and his son had lost money and he was miffed. And he blamed the union. It seems fair to ask who Jack Shields was supposedly representing when he made his public remarks – the public or Jack Shields's bank account? In any event, his remarks drew fire both from Suncor and from the union.

Ryan Moore said Shields was entitled to his opinion, but "we'd prefer to have all discussions to be between the two parties. That's our policy."

And Marchand said while he didn't think having an observer at the meetings was a bad idea, he reminded Shields that the last time they had spoken Shields had suggested Marchand remove himself from the talks and bring in someone else. That's why MIOW brought in Buck Philp, Marchand said.

"Jack Shields must be half-asleep when he's talking to people in his area. He goes out and says one thing one day and another the next."

About the same time, Basken was on a flight one night and saw Jack Shields in a nearby seat. Eavesdropping on Shields' conversation, he heard the MP saying "how the union was destroying McMurray. He said that we were dishonest and destructive and destroying the city. Later, Mike Supple and I had several calls from Shields, and Mike asked, 'How do we treat Shields?' I said, 'Tell Jack Shields to keep his nose out of it. The best thing he can do is say nothing.' I understand that Mike told him there was no role for him. Now my feeling is that the role he wanted to play is that he wanted to get rid of MIOW and ECWU. Shields was mad at me for not wanting him involved. He called me in Hamilton one night (in the latter stages of the dispute). He wanted to be a mediator."

Next to speak up was Norm Weiss who said that it was "about time the MIOW representatives woke up to the reality of the situation" and got back to negotiations. He was duly ignored and the tense waiting went on.

Meanwhile, MIOW members began meeting with school board officials to appeal to them to defer school fees for supplies and for bussing until the dispute ended. All of the schools agreed to be flexible. MIOW members also approached minor hockey officials to work a deal on late payment of hockey fees. There again, they found sympathy and a willingness to defer the fees.

Now, however, another wave of rumours swept the community. This time the rumours focused on benefits Don Marchand was receiving. The rumours received such wide circulation that MIOW eventually issued a press release to deny what everybody was talking about.

"No, our executive and negotiating committee have not received any pay throughout the labour dispute except for the lock-out pay which is available to all our members," the press release read. "No, Mr. Marchand is not the owner of a Cadillac, new or used, nor is he expecting to own one in the future. No, Mr. Marchand has not been promised a job with the ECWU nor has anyone else in our organization and, no, the ECWU is not holding up a settlement with Suncor, they are only providing the resources that enable the MIOW to make responsible decisions."

A day later the Labour Relations Board announced that it was dismissing Suncor's complaint. In its written ruling the board said the evidence presented did not demonstrate that the union had violated the labour relations act. The decision was greeted with a great, collective sigh of relief. But the conclusion didn't say it all. There was an unexpected sting in the written decision. Although the board dismissed the complaint, the ruling noted that the union had not been completely frank with the membership about the back-to-work agreement.

"We are inclined to view these mis-statements over the back-to-work agreement as exhibiting a degree of foolishness, unreasonableness or even of negligence on the part of the union's representatives that we would prefer not to have occurred."

That statement was widely quoted and it was used by the growing number of dissidents to flail away at the negotiating team. For a time, it must have seemed like the ruling had actually gone against them. And added to that critical comment was the finger-wagging final remark the board had made in its written decision: "Neither party is all right or all wrong. Perhaps our hearing will have had some therapeutic effect, and the parties, armed with the additional understanding of each other's position that was gleaned during our hearing, can now take appropriate steps to settle their differences."

Two days later, on September 10, four-and-a-half months after the start of the dispute, a *Fort McMurray Express* headline barked out front page news that seemed to bathe the city in sunlight. "MIOW AGREES TO SUNCOR TERMS" ran the main headline. "Two Issues Remain," the subhead shouted. The story underneath was thin and short.

"In a dramatic move toward settling the four-month Suncor labour dispute, the MIOW has agreed to the company's major financial demands," the story read. "'Economic issues are no longer a major factor,' says MIOW spokesperson John Morrison. 'The only economic factor that is an issue is the time frame.'"

Suncor reacted cautiously to the story. Company officials invited the union to a meeting five days later. Everybody was careful and non-committal; it seemed that the only enthusiasm for the union comment was coming from the ever unpredictable press. Clearly something had happened or was happening. There was movement, but was it glacial in pace or was it an avalanche gathering speed?

Just when private, secret hopes had begun taking root deep within optimistic souls, the company threw freezing water over the news. Nine people who had been convicted of various acts of vandalism during the course of the dispute were handed dismissal letters. The union was talking cooperation and the company answered with a body blow. The reaction was immediate. Two Suncor managers had their cars splashed with paint. A sulphur truck and a taxi were stoned going across the line. Then a large group of union members attempted to block scabs and company staffers from boarding a bus on Silin Forest Road. The RCMP were called but the incident ended without any arrests.

Both sides met two days after the rash of incidents, and the union was in a bellicose mood.

"The union's unconditional surrender is not an acceptable solution to this dispute," MIOW's Gary Morrison told the press. It seemed both sides were back to square one. A wave of disbelief and angry frustration swept across the city. Now a group of MIOW wives called a meeting to discuss ways to bring the dispute to an end. About forty wives turned out for the first meeting, and it quickly emerged that the women were divided into two factions. One group wanted to picket Marchand's house and the office where Suncor's negotiating team were holed up. The other faction insisted that they needed to demonstrate support for the union. One of the meetings ended within ten minutes. Shortly afterward, the wives who wished to demonstrate support for MIOW announced they were organizing another march down Franklin Avenue. And at the same time, the MIOW member who had testified at the Labour Board inquiry revealed himself as one of the organizers of a petition to force another vote on Suncor's last contract offer.

Now the dissidents were surfacing and the debate within the union became a public debate. It was shrill and frantic and triggered massive mood shifts within the community. Then, suddenly, as the din was becoming deafening, Mike Supple and Reg Basken issued a joint press release that silenced everyone.

We have been holding private talks, Basken and Supple stated in the release, and are now encouraging our respective sides to head back to the bargaining table.

"There is light at the end of the tunnel," Wayne Antler said, when asked to comment on the release.

"This is the hottest thing that has happened in getting negotiations on the way again."

A good scare is worth more to a man than good advice.

EDGAR WATSON HOWE

The Great Canadian Oils Sands Suncor plant is located outside of Fort McMurray. Opened in 1967, it was the first oil sands mine and refinery in Alberta.

OVERLEAF: Speaking before the press, labour leaders discuss the situation. (From l to r) Dave Werland, president of the Alberta Federation of Labour; Don Marchand, president of the McMurray Independent Oil Workers Union; Reg Baskin, president of the Energy and Chemical Workers Union; Kerry Woolard, Canadian Labour Congress representative; Ian Thorn, national representative for the Energy and Chemical Workers Union.

CHAPTER TEN

THE DEAL

BASKEN AND SUPPLE had begun meeting after the Labour Board ruling. Basken says he was still testy about the complaint Suncor had filed and he says he was blunt when he first got together with Supple.

"I said to Supple, 'I know you have three choices: 1. Recognize ECWU and negotiate an agreement; 2. Make a deal behind our back with MIOW and run us off the property; 3. Get rid of both of us and offer the members work without the union.' I repeated that a number of times, up to and including the last hours before the settlement. It wasn't clear he agreed. He didn't say that he agreed. He just made no comment on the alternatives. I did most of the talking and I said of the alternatives, there's only one you can use. I requested a meeting with Suncor's Board of Directors. I said, 'Mike, if you don't go to the Board of Directors and re-commend the only alternative that will work for you – to negotiate a deal with us – then I want to go to the Board of Directors myself and tell them why they should do that.' He said something to the effect, 'I hear you.' He knew I wasn't bluffing. I told him we had $6 million in the strike fund and that if I gave it all to MIOW it would make his life so damn miserable he would wish he had taken the proper alternative. I also told him that they would never get rid of MIOW because we would support MIOW."

From the final days of September, while the anger and quarrelling and picket line incidents escalated in Fort McMurray, to the end of the first week of October, Basken and Supple met daily. They concentrated on the issues and left aside the question of whether Suncor was actually prepared to accept the presence of an ECWU affiliate at the plant.

After ten days of talks, says Basken, he felt he had "a final understanding that the terms and conditions that we were putting on the settlement were terms and conditions that Suncor could accept. The only thing that was outstanding was whether Suncor would accept them without a union at all or with just MIOW or with us as well. That was never finalized."

With the understanding he had worked out with Supple, Basken and the MIOW negotiating team began preparing for a meeting with the membership to put the offer to a vote. But Basken was uneasy, was still uncertain about what Suncor management had in mind.

"During the weekend before the ratification meeting," Basken says, "we got wind that printing companies in Fort McMurray were working overtime printing documents for Suncor. At that point, I had the very strong opinion that the documents were going to be an offer to return to work without the union and without MIOW. And that they would be used just prior to our ratification meeting and they'd throw the whole thing out the window. I was convinced at the time that the membership wouldn't take it. So I phoned Supple at home on the weekend. I was in Ottawa. He had not yet gotten approval from his Board of Directors. The board meeting was Monday. If they went for the agreement, that meant they were recognizing the union. Remember the parties hated each other for twenty years. When Supple and the negotiating team agreed with us, we knew they would have to get higher company approval. I can't remember whether the memo had been signed. I don't think we had their ink on the document yet, but we had the agreement that these were the terms and conditions. The way things work, if they have signed, then you have a memorandum. If they haven't signed, then you have a different purpose for the meeting. When I phoned Supple on the Saturday I told him I wanted to go to the board meeting Monday. I told him I knew there were documents being printed in Fort McMurray, and I cautioned him not to distribute anything. He never admitted to anything. I have no proof but I still suspect I am correct. I told him I was staying at the Hilton in Ottawa. I said, 'I'll check for messages every hour through Sunday and I want to know if you are going to prevent me from going to the Board of Directors meeting.' And I said, 'Cause I'll get to them afterwards if you make the wrong decision. The only thing acceptable to me is that you are going to the board to recommend acceptance. Anything else is a double-cross and I'll be very unhappy. And you won't win.' There was a lot of silence. Then some back and forth."

All day Sunday Basken checked for messages and as the hours ticked off his nervous tension coiled ever tighter. Finally, "late Sunday afternoon I got a call from Supple's secretary. My blood pressure went up. When she said 'hello' she said, 'Hello Reg' and not 'Mr. Basken.' And her tone. She asked if I would have breakfast with Supple in Edmonton at the Chateau Lacombe on Tuesday morning at seven. Her tone said he was going to the Board of Directors and that he was going to recommend acceptance. That was just my sense. If he was going to recommend otherwise he likely wouldn't have wanted to be in the same room with me. I am sure I can holler louder and I would have."

Tuesday morning Basken said he arrived "early for breakfast and as Supple walked across the floor it was obvious to me he was recommending the right thing. I think we shook within two minutes."

The following day, October 8, Basken issued the press release in which he announced that he and Supple had reached an understanding on all the contested issues in the dispute. Suncor wouldn't comment that day but Basken said both negotiating committees were to meet to settle final details. Basken wouldn't reveal what he had won or had given away on MIOW's behalf. Still, his press release made the front pages and many union members were prepared to accept, by then, pretty much any agreement that didn't mean major rollbacks, layoffs or the disappearance of the union.

Over the next few days both negotiating teams met and then MIOW arranged for a meeting with the membership on October 13. More than 600 members of MIOW attended the meeting and, after having the offer explained to them, 79.6 per cent voted to accept. Marchand walked out of the meeting and told reporters that the new contract was worth the five-and-a-half-month lockout.

"Both the company and the union understand how hard things are for both sides and I think that this will bring both sides closer together. There are a lot of new things in the contract like the dialoguing agreement, which is good for everybody provided that the dialoguing goes both ways."

Suncor spokesman Wayne Antler said the company was pleased with the vote and happy to have MIOW members back at work.

The details of the agreement were made public the following day. Wages were frozen and overtime pay was reduced to time-and-a-half until November 1987. It would then return to double time. Wages would also be increased if Suncor's financial situation improved the following year. The nine employees who were dismissed for picket line incidents were rehired, although some were suspended for short periods. The apprentices who had been laid off were rehired. And, finally, the layoff procedures and severance packages were improved slightly. It was a hold-the-line agreement, and although it was criticized by many, it seemed a pretty significant achievement given the panic that was gripping the entire industry as a result of the free-fall of oil prices.

Basken says throughout his discussions with Supple he kept repeating that ECWU was going to save Suncor "$500,000 in the first year in labour relations costs. And because there was no wage increase in the settlement, I said, 'That money is going to the membership. That's for the first year. After that you get to keep the money.' I said, 'We are going to have a joint training session for stewards and supervisors. We are going to do some things differently.' Marchand didn't agree (with the $500,000 provision) so we crossed it out of the agreement but I told Supple, 'We crossed it out but it's still there. Do you read me?' He said, 'Ya, ya.' And the deal was that we'd send our accountant to check their figures at year end."

Supple too talked to the press after the vote and he was both frank and hopeful.

"This dispute was aimed at improving a very bad working climate here," he told *Fort McMurray Express* in an interview.

"I think it was too complex an issue to get serious treatment from the media. A lot of people didn't understand the basics of the disagreement...So we committed on management side to improve our performance on the handling of grievances and dealing with our employees and listening to them and we also sought some requirements on the union side by which they would train their stewards and make other commitments to work together."

Asked to identify the biggest change in labour/management relations that occurred during the dispute, Supple said that it was "the intervention of the ECWU. That brings a lot more know-how and skill to the table."

And finally, asked whether Suncor had planned to break the union, Supple said the company had "entered the dispute with all our plans laid out to react to whatever the outcome was. It is true to say we were prepared for all possible scenarios. I'm not going to go further than that. (However) I must emphasize our preference has always been to have our bargaining unit employees come back to work through a cooperative labour/management agreement."

Ef you want peace, the thing you've gut to do is jes' to show you're up to fightin', tu.

JAMES RUSSELL LOWELL

Sam John giving the thumbs up sign as he takes part in the march down Franklin Avenue.

OVERLEAF: MIOW workers celebrate their aquittal of charges laid at the Suncor plant gate. (From l to r) Dan Boreen, Dwayn Martychuk, Mike Pearson, Jim Malcolm, unknown, Reg Moss, unknown.

CONCLUSION

MIOW MEMBERS began returning to work on October 24. Although 1100 had been locked out, only about 800 returned to the jobs they had previously held. More than 150 had sent in formal resignations and the others had, presumably, found work elsewhere and moved on without saying goodbye. Both Marchand and Wood had written letters to the members and to the supervisors encouraging everyone to let bygones be bygones. But the wounds were fresh, and inevitably, there were clashes.

Alvin Norman says he was eager to get back to work but took with him a deep, gnawing anger.

"I remember this millwright stayed in (on the job). We had been pretty good friends. The first night back I walked around the ball mill just to have a look and he came around the other side and he extended his hand to me. I just flipped out and told him where to stick that hand. I said, 'Just don't even talk to me, just stay away from me, don't even look me in the face.' That was the end of it. We never spoke and he never stayed long after. To me it just came back to the family. They had attacked my family. You can do whatever you want with me but don't touch my family. I think if I had gotten another job in that first year I would have left. I didn't have any loyalties. But time heals everything. I don't feel the same. It doesn't bother me as much anymore."

Keith Barrington had been arrested during the dispute and charged for a rock throwing incident. Now president of the local, he says he was one of the nine who were fired, then rehired. He received a three-month suspension and didn't make it back to work until January.

"I was bitter about it, but really I got over it relatively fast. I was vocal and radical on the picket line. I was a good employee before lockout began. I went to work after the three-month sus-pension and have had no problems since...My knowledge of strikes was that you did whatever you had to to stop other people from doing your job. I don't believe that any more. My involvement in the union has changed my attitude."

Brian Campbell said for him it was "a relief to go back to work and get a regular paycheque. I didn't go back with any ani-mosity toward any party at all. We all changed in 1986. We all had to. In 1986, I decided enough is enough. I had to make a decision in my own mind either go back to work and accept it, go back to work and sulk for the rest of my life or quit. So I decided to accept it. I've always been a worker. I always will be. So I went back and did my job. I enjoy my work. I always have. I don't like scabs. And certainly the employer hired a lot of them on after 1986. Which I think is a major mistake on the employer's part. Employers use people in times like that. When they have finished with them a lot of employers just throw them away. Suncor hired many and created some tough times on our site. But I took the position that they were in the union, and we'd be better off trying to make good union people out of them rather than trying to disrupt their lives."

Jimmy Cardinal said there were "a few scabs on staff when we went back. I didn't treat them bad. To this day I got friends who hold grudges. In 1978, Catalytic employees (who were contracted to Suncor), did not cross our line. In 1986, because of their contract, they had to cross. Me, I can't hold it against them. There were guys that quit Catalytic because they didn't want to cross the line. There were certain people who were true-blue union."

But Cardinal wasn't able to expunge all of his hard feelings. One memory rankled.

"This one guy, I saw him down at The Brick one time three years after the dispute. I remember him giving me the finger as he crossed the line. All I did (when he crossed) was I told him, 'Hey, back us up.' And he gave me the finger. He was just a tiny guy and he drove this big truck. So I see him at The Brick. I walked up to him and I said, 'You're not all that big when you are not behind the wheel.' He said, 'I don't know you.' I said, 'Oh, yes you do. You know me. I know you partner.' I said, 'Why don't you give me the finger now. For a little guy I don't know why you showed off that much in 1986.' I said, 'If I could have found you in 1986 you wouldn't be walking around here today.' I said, 'I think you better leave before you piss me off.' And he was gone."

Bill Johnston, who in 1994 said he still holds a grudge against scabs who were hired on, and still won't shop at local stores that didn't support MIOW, was annoyed when he returned to work to find "the place was in pretty bad shape. They broke into lockers and stole stuff. They told us before it started that we could leave stuff in our lockers. But they stole stuff from my locker."

Kerry Wood, Ron Wood's daughter, says she actually voted against the final agreement. She says she just didn't think it was a good deal. The lockout had been a rough ride for her personally. Two months into the dispute she began getting a number of threatening calls – one caller threatened to burn her house down. She told him to go ahead. What angered her was that the caller, she suspected, was in all likelihood a so-called union brother who thought he could get to her dad through her.

"It was very tense going back. A lot of people complained about the money they lost," she said.

Peggy Colclough, who now works in the union office, says that first Christmas after the return to work was "pretty bleak for us. One day we were down at the arena and this woman came in with a gorgeous fur coat. I said, 'You were pretty lucky. Your husband must have been good to you for Christmas.' She turned to me, knowing that Larry was a union member, and said, 'You can thank MIOW for this.' Her husband was a staffer. He worked throughout the lockout. I just walked away. To this day, I can't speak to her."

Peggy says it took a long time for many families to recover financially.

"It took the average family about two years. There were six months of mortgage payments to catch up on. That's at least $6,000. Plus, some people maybe lost their cars. And got a poor credit rating. Some people are still feeling the pinch. There are still people who are bitter, union members who won't talk to the bus drivers."

One of the most poignant stories about friendships damaged during the dispute came from Cal Morrison.

"I lost a real good friendship with a supervisor who worked in top shop. We haven't been the same since. A year before I went to Suncor I worked for this guy. He had a trucking company. We got along great. He was a member of the Operating Engineers Union. He always warned me never to cross a picket line with the truck when we'd be talking about going to different job sites. When the lockout started and his company folded I went to visit him one day. He wasn't home and his wife told me he was in Edmonton, that he'd be home that night. The next day he wasn't back when I called. Then I found out he was working at Suncor. I called him one night and I called him all sorts of names. Then about a year ago my son got burned in an accident at Suncor. He was in the burn unit of the University of Alberta Hospital. I was down there and I needed somebody to talk to and I called up (the ex-friend who had scabbed). He'd moved to Edmonton by then. Jesus, he offered me a car and a place to stay. And the next thing I knew he and his wife were both down there at the hospital. He was a friend when I needed one. We aren't as close as we were before. Now he admits he made a mistake but he says, 'You don't realize, I was up against it, bad off.'"

Within the business community there had been many casualties and it would take years for the city to recover. One of the most prominent financial collapses was the little business empire that MP Jack Shields had built. His local holdings included Redwood Ready Mix, Garden Café, Smitty's Restaurant, Bucketwheel Restaurant, Dairy Queen and an interest in his son's failed restaurant, O'Reilly's.

Shields said his firm's plunge into receivership was like "a death in the family." He blamed the failure on the lockout, on low oil prices and on the collapse of an Edmonton bank.

Even longer lasting than the financial damage done to the community was the psychological hurt inflicted. Many people carried anger with them for years afterward. Perhaps one of the most bizarre incidents related, if only tangentially, to the dispute occurred in 1991. A thirty-nine-year-old cab driver was charged in March of that year with the brutal murder of a fifteen-year-old girl. The cabby, who was found guilty and sentenced to life, was suffering from paranoid delusional disorder at the time of the killing. At his trial it was revealed that he had convinced himself that the girl was part of a dark conspiracy by Suncor union members to kill him for taking a passenger across the picket line in 1986.

The point of that tragic tale is that conflict claims its own victims, some directly, others by indirect and even glancing blows. Who knows what caused the cabby's mental problems. In his deluded state he managed to connect his mental suffering to a conflict that had torn the city apart five years earlier. There may not have been any connection other than the fact that he had lived in Fort McMurray at the time. He had been enveloped in the air of crisis like everyone else. Where others managed to come to terms with what it had meant or had done to their lives, he had done otherwise. He had incorporated it into his fantasy life. And a fifteen-year-old girl lost her life because of it.

Despite the string of tragedies that the dispute engendered there was, is, a happy ending. The dispute allowed a river of accumulated grit to work itself out of labour relations at the plant. Years of mutual distrust, of personality conflicts, of bad management and of sloppy work habits had ground away at every point of labour/management contact. The two sides could barely talk to each other by the early 1980s. Almost six months on the line helped flush out many of the irritants. By the time MIOW members went back in, everything had been restructured. They were now part of a national union, they were receiving training both in contract negotiations and in how to be effective stewards. Management likewise rid itself of supervisors who had been identified as problems and retrained the ones who were kept on. Both sides began to trust each other and collaborate in running the plant and mine with greater efficiency and safety. Company and senior union officials began meeting regularly to discuss problems in the plant.

The results of the new relationship were evident within a matter of months. Where 357 grievances had been filed in 1985, a mere 17 were filed in 1987. Sick time dropped precipitously and so did overtime. At the same time, production costs began falling and production rates rising. The changes were so dramatic and so immediate that six months after the return to work, Supple called Basken to make good on his promise.

"Supple phoned me and told me we had to check on that $500,000," Basken recalls. The deal was, if MIOW saved Suncor $500,000 in labour relations costs in the first year, Supple would give the money to the union members. ECWU was to send up an accountant to check the company's figures.

"So I sent Buck (Philp) up and called him an accountant," says Basken. "Buck phoned me after he got up there and said, 'Reg, sorry they didn't save $500,000.' I said, 'Those rotten bastards. Marchand was right. They're lying.' Buck said, 'Oh shut up. They saved $750,000 and they are sending a check out for $750 to every member.' Well Marchand said, 'Don't cash the cheque, they didn't pay the income tax on it. I said, 'Cash it before they change their minds.' So everybody got $750. It was just a continuation of Marchand's anger at the company. He had every right to be. The company had treated him like shit and he had treated them like shit. It had been fertilizer personified. A fight is a wonderful thing except most people don't go to work to have a fight."

Once the major problems had been ironed out at the plant, MIOW members voted on their affiliation with ECWU. Grateful for the $1.5 million-plus that ECWU had given them in strike pay and impressed with the expertise of the larger union, they voted to merge and become a local of ECWU. Marchand hung on for another year as president an finally resigned in September, 1987. A month later, Dan Comrie was elected president. Marchand had been an inspiring war chief, but had difficulty adapting to the new spirit of management relations. Shortly after his resignation Marchand decided to leave Fort McMurray. He says his doctor told him he was burned-out and that if he kept going at the same pace, "he'd have to reserve a room for me at the Royal Alexandra Hospital in Edmonton."

Ron Wood said Marchand's decision to leave came as no surprise.

"I'll be very frank about it. I was happy to see him go from his union position. But socially, Don and I got along really well. He contributed to the community. But from a management perspective, it was good that he left. He got an early retirement."

Marchand is now living in BC and working as a car salesman. Wood also retired shortly after and now lives in Calgary. He fishes, golfs and works as a hockey scout for the Fort McMurray Oil Barons.

Graham and Colleen Waterman (at centre) take part in the march through Fort McMurray.

ACKNOWLEDGEMENTS

I SPENT A HAPPY SUMMER in Alberta researching the 1986 Suncor lockout. I was moved by the stories I heard and during my trip north I learned a great deal about Alberta labor politics and about Fort McMurray. I had been in the city years before chasing news as a cub reporter for *The Edmonton Journal.* I have vivid recollections of trailing the minister responsible for workplace safety, Bill Diachuk, around the city, and asking him why he had chosen to fly to Fort McMurray to investigate complaints about lax safety standards at the Suncor plant at a time when the entire facility had been shut down for maintenance. I also recall he didn't talk to a single worker during his visit. In his own way, Bill taught me a great deal about reporting and about how the story is not always what the minister says it is.

Many people kindly gave of their time and showed great patience in explaining things to me. Thanks to Ian Thorn, Peggy Colclough, Alvin Norman and the others in the union office. I would also like to thank those who consented to interviews: Don Marchand, Carl Cullihall, Bill Ross, Bill and Edna Johnston, Deb York, Dave Scott, Brian Campbell, Cal Morrison, Larry Colclough, Jimmy Cardinal, Kirk McRae, Keith Barrington, Brian McFalls,

Kerry Wood, Jed Matthews, Raymond and Pamela Lays, Ian Thorn, and Ed and Jeanette Stacy. Darrell Skidnuk, managing editor of *Fort McMurray Today*, graciously parted with some of the photos that appear in this book. When we met, he was welcoming and curious about the project. Thanks as well to *Today* reporter Patrick Nichol who alerted me to the story of the mad cabby.

In Edmonton, Sheila Greckol, Dan Comrie and Gary Shury filled in many important details. Back in Ottawa, Reg Baskin gave me an overview of the lockout.

I'd also like to thank Gene Bacon and Ron Wood for speaking so frankly about their roles in the dispute and for offering me a management perspective. Allan Askeland of Diversified Transport also deserves thanks for relating some of his experiences with labour strife at the Suncor plant.

Finally, Jean Poulin, the ultimate authority at Duval House Publishing, brought enthusiasm to this project, and I must thank him for talking me into writing it.